A Handbook for

The Freemason's Wife

Philippa Faulks
and Cheryl Skidmore

A Handbook for

The Freemason's Wife

Philippa Faulks
and Cheryl Skidmore

Lewis Masonic

Acknowledgements

Many people helped contribute to the creation of this book, and we would like to extend our sincere thanks to the following: our publisher, Lewis Masonic, for their insight to include this title in their list; editor Jay Slater for his patience and support; Keith Wootton for his design and, of course, the production team.

Appreciation and thanks as always to our agent Fiona Spencer Thomas.

Our sincere thanks go to the United Grand Lodge of England for granting us permission to use their Freemasonry Q & A; to Trevor McKeown from Freemasonry.bcy.ca for his great help in providing images for the book; to Robert L. D. Cooper for the beautiful images of the 'Three Graces' and the 'Cardinal Virtues'; thanks to *Freemasonry Today*, also to Ian Simpson at the TLC Appeal for his support and help with the charity information. Many thanks also to the following charities for providing information and images: the Royal Masonic Benevolent Institution, the Royal Masonic Trust for Girls & Boys, MSF, Grand Charity, Ireland Masons and Cumbrian West Masons. Special thanks to Mrs Margaret McGhee for allowing us to reproduce her poem and in memory of George Power (deceased) for the extracts from *A Masonic Miscellany*. Grateful appreciation is to all Masons who offered information and support for this project – we couldn't have done it without you!

Last but definitely not least, our love and thanks go to our husbands and families who have given us unstinting support throughout, especially to Andrew for his sterling work creating many of the images.

First published 2009
Reprinted 2010

ISBN 978 0 85318 313 6

Published by Lewis Masonic
an imprint of Ian Allan Publishing Ltd., Hersham, Surrey KT12 4RG

Printed in England by Ian Allan Printing Ltd., Hersham, Surrey KT12 4RG

Distributed in the United States of America and Canada by BookMasters Distribution Services.

Contents

Introduction

Have you ever wondered why men want to be Freemasons? How do they become one and what does it involve?

Everyone has heard at least one thing about the Masons, whether it is good or bad, but what is the truth?

As the wives of two well-established Freemasons, we aim to give you a simple and straight-to-the-point guide to the basics of Freemasonry. We can steer you through the initially bemusing concepts until you have a clear understanding of the path of moral learning your men folk will be involved in. We will demystify the myths and put paid to the rumours and in doing so make you feel reassured, more knowledgeable and respectful of a wonderful Craft.

Whether you are the girlfriend, wife, partner or close relation of a Freemason or Freemason-to-be, you will find within this book the answer to almost every question you will ever need to know about Freemasonry. From the initial queries on becoming a Mason, to the role of Lady at Ladies' Night, the answers and suggestions are here.

For the purpose of simplicity we have tended to use the terms 'wife' and 'husband' throughout the book. This obviously does not imply that all Freemasons are married, nor indeed that this book is intended purely for the wives. We hope that it will be of great use not only to the wives, girlfriends and partners, but to the families and friends of potential or long-standing Freemasons. We have also included a list of Masonic terminology which may be of use to you on your journey through the book. We have light-heartedly termed it 'Mason-speak'.

Basic Mason-speak

Candidate	a Mason-to-be
Brethren	fellow Masons
Lodge	an assembly of Masons
Temple	the room where the Masonic rituals are held
The Craft	refers to Lodges that work the Three Degrees as outlined in the constitutions of the Grand Lodge of England
The Three Degrees	the three rituals the Mason must work through to become a Master Mason
Ritual	a moral play acted out in the Temple
Initiation	the first ritual to be encountered by the new candidate
Entered Apprentice	the title given to the new Mason when the First Degree (initiation) has occurred
Fellow Craft	the title given to the apprentice when he has passed the Second Degree
Master Mason	the title given when the Fellow Craft has achieved the Third Degree
Festive Board	the meal after the Lodge meeting
Worshipful Master	the ruler of the Lodge
Supreme Being/ Great Architect of the Universe	members are required to believe in a god, energy or principle that is of a superior and positive nature. The terminology is there to reinforce the lack of religious connotation or dogma; it does not imply a specific god or an attempt to combine all gods into one.
Regalia	the 'uniform' of a Freemason indicating rank
Apron	item of regalia worn by all Freemasons
On the Square	a reference to being a Mason
On the Level	another reference to being a Mason, indicating he is a good, balanced man
Officers of the Lodge	a gradual progression of positions held within the Lodge. See Chapter 3

Mother Lodge	the particular Lodge where first made a Mason
Lodge of Instruction (LOI)	provides those who wish to or who hold office the chance to rehearse ritual under the instruction of experienced Brethren
Blue Lodge	the term for Craft Freemasonry widely used in the United States believed to refer to the colour of regalia traditionally used in Freemasonry originating from England and Ireland
Royal Arch	a Master Mason may join this Lodge which complements (or some say 'completes') the three Craft degrees
Chapter	another name for Royal Arch
In the Chair	when you become Worshipful Master
Lewis	the son of a Mason

A Mason and a Man

My Brother, Masonry means much more
Than the wearing of a pin.
Or carrying a paid-up dues receipt
So the Lodge will let you in.

You may wear an emblem on your coat
From your finger flash a ring
But if you're not sincere at heart
This doesn't mean a thing.

It's merely an outward sign to show
The world that you belong
To this great fraternal brotherhood
That teaches right from wrong.

What really counts lies buried deep
Within the human breast
Till Masonic teaching brings it out
And puts it to the test.

If you practise out of Lodge
The things that you learn within
Be just and upright to yourself
And to your fellow men.

Console a brother when he's sick
And assist him when in need
Without a thought of personal reward
For any act or deed.

Walk and act in such a way
That the world without can see
That only the best can meet the test
Laid down by Masonry.

Be always faithful to your trust
And do the best that you can
Then you can proudly tell the world
You're a Mason and a man.

— Author unknown

1

So he wants to be a Freemason?

I Dearly Love a Mason.
American Postcard. The
Ullman Manufacturing
Company, New York 1909.
Author's Collection

What is Freemasonry?
Who can become a Freemason?
How do you become a Freemason?
What do they do?

These are the main questions most people initially ask when the subject arises. In this and further chapters we aim to provide you with simple answers to these and other frequently asked questions. We hope that in doing so we can help dispel some of the myths and rumours that surround Freemasonry, the largest and oldest fraternity in the world. Members have included kings, presidents, prime ministers, judges, admirals, generals, top businessmen, film stars, sportsmen, composers and most importantly, ordinary folk from all walks of life.

* denotes Q&As reproduced by kind permission of the United Grand Lodge of England

Q: What is Freemasonry?

A: Freemasonry under the United Grand Lodge of England (UGLE) is the UK's largest fraternal and charitable organisation. It has over 300,000 members working in nearly 8,000 Lodges throughout England and Wales and 30,000 more members overseas. It is entirely secular, allowing men of any social group, race or religion to join. It teaches moral lessons through a series of allegorical plays and learning, known as the Three Degrees. It is also the largest contributor to charity in the world, offering financial support to a huge variety of charities and individuals. It is not a religion nor a rival to nor substitute for any religion. It is not a secret society: the only secrets are the handshakes, signs and passwords, rather like using a personal identity number or PIN to identify oneself when visiting other Lodges. It is not a political group: discussion of politics and religion is banned during meetings. It discourages intolerance and prejudice in all forms. Freemasonry offers no financial reward nor does it encourage any form of nepotism or obligation to other members in any ordinary business relations. Its principles do not conflict with members' duties as citizens; in fact it should strengthen their personal responsibilities in both their public and private lives. Freemasonry also demands that its members show respect for the law and religion of the country they reside in.

Q: Who can become a Freemason?

A: A man of mature age, normally 21 years old, but in some circumstances admission may be given to younger men, i.e. sons/close male relatives of a Freemason. He must be of good report, that is, has committed no serious crime or has a reputation for immoral actions etc, and has a belief in a Supreme Being.

Q: How do you become a Freemason?

A: This can be threefold:
- wait until you are asked by another Mason
- ask another Mason
- or simply apply to the United Grand Lodge of your country.

'Three Principles or Virtues'. Lee Woodward Zeigler. *Mackey's History of Freemasonry*, New York & London 1906

The next steps are:

Application – either through personal recommendation by a proposer or via application from United Grand Lodge or Provincial Grand Lodge (usually each county has one). Then a form can be filled in and submitted to your chosen Lodge.

Interview – the next step will be to have an interview with the Lodge, when they will vote to see whether they think the applicant is a suitable candidate, i.e. that he is a law-abiding and respectable member of society. Some Lodges will also organise a home visit to chat to the wife/partner/family of the proposed Mason to explain many of the points we are covering here.

The final step is for the members of the Lodge to hold a ballot. They vote using a system of white and black balls. If there are two black balls in the ballot box, the proposed member has been rejected (this is where the term being 'blackballed' comes from). This however is almost unheard of because if there are any objections to a proposed candidate, members are encouraged to discreetly raise the issue with the appropriate Brethren before the ballot takes place.

Q: What do they do?
A: Freemasonry encourages the progression of moral and spiritual values, so that the men involved may become better men in all roles in their lives. The Freemason is taught a series of lessons through ritual dramas known as the Three Degrees (see Chapter 2 – The Craft). Each meeting involves one of these rituals as each member progresses through his respective degrees. After each meeting is a Festive Board where the Masons gather for a meal, speeches and occasionally a lecture on Freemasonry. The members are encouraged to offer what they can afford towards the current charity they are supporting (often called the Master's List) by organising a raffle or just passing a contribution box around. Freemasons follow the *Three Great Principles*: Brotherly Love, Relief and Truth, which we will explain below.

The Three Great Principles

Brotherly Love – to show tolerance and respect for the opinions of others and to behave always with kindness and understanding to all fellow creatures.

Relief – to practise charity and to care not only for your own, but for the community as a whole. This may be achieved by charitable giving or voluntary work as a group or an individual.

Truth – to strive always for truth and high moral standards and apply them in all aspects of life.

Why become a Freemason?
People are often bemused as to why men want to join Freemasonry as opposed to what they would perhaps term other 'clubs'. It is for a variety of reasons. Each individual may have different feelings, but here are a few examples:

Self improvement – simply to strive to become a better man in all areas of life. The progression through the offices of the Lodge also gives the Mason confidence and a sense of achievement and a desire to prove himself worthy of the trust of his Brethren and peers. Freemasonry also provides a positive channel for the male 'pack' or 'herd' instinct: the need to belong to something. The moral lessons and principles offered by Freemasonry can help give the Mason the skills to be a better husband/father/provider/etc.

Quest for knowledge – Freemasonry intrigues many people, whether it is its history, origins and/or the mystery surrounding it.

Skills – learning a variety of skills from others within the order (i.e. speechmaking, memorisation of ritual), gaining organisational and social skills, obtaining wisdom from peers and/or having a mentor.

Charity – as one of the world's largest contributors to charity, members feel that it is an honourable and worthwhile organisation to belong to. It allows people to feel that they are able to give something back substantially to the community. Two wonderful examples of Masonic charitable giving to their local community are as follows:

The family of a young girl suffering from cystic fibrosis and waiting for a heart and lung transplant was given the financial assistance by a local Masonic Lodge to purchase a portable heart defibrillator to keep at home. She was so ill that at any moment she could go into cardiac arrest and need to be revived. The equipment ensured that she was able to live long enough to have her transplant.

A small country school was deemed by inspectors to lack the necessary building and equipment standards to allow it to stay open. The local Lodge members took it upon themselves to offer their monetary and skilled services as builders, electricians, etc. They built a new extension and provided curricular supplies. The school then passed the next inspection and was actually given a certificate of excellence.

Whenever there has been a national or international emergency such as the 9/11 terrorist attacks on the World Trade Center in New York or the Boxing Day Tsunami, the Masons have often been the first to discreetly offer their financial aid. Other well supported causes are local hospices, children's charities and air ambulance services. Freemasons do not advertise their charitable donations and so often we are unaware of their generosity, even in our local communities.

Not all the money raised by Freemasons goes to non-Masonic causes. Chapter 6 discusses the Masonic charities which exist to help elderly, sick or impoverished Masons and the widows of deceased Freemasons.

A sense of brotherhood – it allows people from all walks of life to meet and work together and be equal. There may be a dustman seated next to a Lord, or a brain surgeon next to a foreman of a factory: in Freemasonry all men are perceived as equal. There may be men as young as 21 and those as old as 90; there will be men of all nationalities and religions such as Muslims, Jews, Sikhs, Christians or Hindus. This exciting variety of members encourages tolerance and a broad mind.

The Lodge Where I Belong

Though my lodge may lack the splendour
Of a Temple or a Shrine,
Or possess the gaudy fixtures
That are classed as superfine,
Yet the fellowship it offers
Is in price beyond compare.
And I wouldn't trade it ever
For life's treasures, rich or fair!

The hand-clasp firm, the word of cheer,
Oh, such meanings they impart,
The mysteries of brotherhood
That links us heart to heart!
You'd really have to travel far,
For friendships quite so strong
As those one always find right here
In the Lodge where I belong.
When all my earthly travels end,

And at last I'm borne to rest
Where mortals hands no longer toil
And I cease life's endless quest
Why there's nothing I'd like better
Should I join the heavenly throng
Than to meet with all the Brothers
Of the Lodge where I belong.

— *Arthur R. Herrman*

Time and commitments

Many people are understandably concerned with regard to the time and money required to become a Freemason. The proposed member is made fully aware of all monetary costs and obligations to attend Lodge before he makes the commitment to become a Mason and is encouraged to discuss this with his wife/partner and/or family. He should always take into consideration whether they can afford his membership and whether he can spare the necessary time to attend Lodge meetings.
Freemasonry encourages all members to put their families before anything else, whether it is money, time or other commitments. The main costs are as follows:

- Initiation fee
- Annual subscription and dining fees
- Dark suit; a black Provincial or Grand Lodge tie; white gloves and apron. Usually the Lodge will lend you an Entered Apprentice and a Fellow Craft apron and you will then just have to buy a Master Mason's apron.

Q: What will it cost to become a Freemason?
A: Many Lodges have a differing fee, so it is fairly simple to choose one to suit your financial situation. On entry there is an initiation fee to pay. Each member pays an annual subscription to his own Lodge, which covers the cost of membership and administration. After each meeting there is a meal. Some Lodges include dining fees in the subscription, others ask for a separate payment. Again, the amount varies from Lodge to Lodge. Charitable donations are at the discretion of each member and members are encouraged to give only what they can reasonably afford. A Master Mason may join more than one Lodge, but only what he can afford in money and time without detriment to his family or other responsibilities.

Q: How often will he have to go to Lodge?
A: This varies from Lodge to Lodge. Some have meetings once a month, some have only four a year. There is a summer sabbatical for some Lodges between June and September when the Masonic 'season' restarts. If a Mason is a member of several Lodges then his commitment in time and money will increase, but he must always take into account his responsibilities to home and family first.

Q: Will my husband have to remove his wedding ring to be a Freemason?
A: Only for the First Degree. This is a practice which has gained some negative responses from those who do not understand Freemasonry and has led to some unease amongst women who feel that Freemasonry is trying to 'convert' their husbands away from marriage or their faith. It is in no way intended to be symbolic of separation or otherwise interfere with the Mason's bond with his wife. It is in fact a preparation for the First Degree (initiation) whereby the candidate is 'divested of all metals'. It is not just the man's wedding ring that will be removed, it is all articles of a metallic nature – money, jewellery, belt buckles, etc. This reflects the part in the ceremony when the candidate is asked as a good Mason to give to charity. Of course, he has no money or any other metallic substances and is effectively destitute and unable to comply with the request! He is then sternly reminded that being penniless and poor can occur at any point and that he should always strive to help relieve those in distress whenever he is able.

Q: Will I be allowed to go to Lodge?
A: Not for the normal meetings, but there will be Lodge open-days, social events and the annual Ladies' Night, when you will be welcomed with open arms to enjoy a meal and some festivities all in your honour!

Q: Why don't you have women members?*
A: Traditionally, Freemasonry under the United Grand Lodge of England has been restricted to men. The early stonemasons were all male, and when Freemasonry was established in 1717, the position of women in society was different from that of today. If women wish to join Freemasonry, there are two separate Grand Lodges in England restricted to women only.

Q: What will I gain from my husband being a Freemason?
A: You will gain the peace of mind that your husband is being encouraged to put his wife and family always before others and that he is on a path to make him a better man. Freemasonry encourages fidelity towards wives and partners.

Secrets and myths

Q: Is Freemasonry a secret society?*
A: No, but Lodge meetings, like those of many other groups, are private and open only to members. The rules and aims of Freemasonry are available to the public. Meeting places are known and in many areas are used by the local community for activities other than Freemasonry. Members are encouraged to speak openly about Freemasonry.

Q: So what are the secrets of Freemasonry?*
A: The secrets in Freemasonry are the traditional modes of recognition which are not used indiscriminately, but solely as a test of membership, e.g. when visiting a Lodge where you are not known.

Q: Why do some Freemasons wear little pin badges with strange symbols on?
A: Pin badges are often worn to represent the Lodge the Mason belongs to or his position within the Lodge. Freemasonry has a lot of symbolism connected to it and therefore some of the badges may look a bit strange. A common badge is that of

a blue forget-me-not flower. It was originally designed in 1934 so that German Freemasons, who were under serious threat from the Nazis, could still be identified. It was also worn in the concentration camps by those Masons determined to keep the light of Freemasonry alive. This emblem is now worn in honour and remembrance of the Freemasons who were persecuted during World War 2.

Q: Why can't my husband discuss what happens in the Lodge? Is he keeping secrets from me?
A: Freemasons are at liberty to discuss everything except the passwords, signs and other obligations. Often the partners or wives help their husbands to learn their ritual. This is contained in a little blue ritual book (which you will probably become quite acquainted with!) and has everything included except for the passwords and signs. To a non-Mason, the rituals may seem like gibberish and would only mean something in the context of the ceremony, but to the Mason the ritual is a very emotional experience and to begin with he may not fully understand it himself. What you can understand from this is that your husband is on a path to becoming a better man and that is something to admire and feel at peace with.

Q: Why do Freemasons take oaths?*
A: New members make solemn promises concerning their conduct in Lodge and in society. Each member also promises to keep confidential the traditional methods of proving that he is a Freemason which he would use when visiting a Lodge where he is not known. Freemasons do not swear allegiances to each other or to Freemasonry. Freemasons promise to support others in times of need, but only if that support does not conflict with their duties to God, the law, their family or with their responsibilities as a citizen.

Q: Why do your 'obligations' contain hideous penalties?*
A: They no longer do. When Masonic ritual was developing in the late 1600s and 1700s, it was quite common for legal and civil oaths to include physical penalties and Freemasonry simply followed the practice of the times. In Freemasonry, however, the physical penalties were always symbolic and were never carried out. After long discussion, they were removed from the promises in 1986.

Q: Are Freemasons expected to prefer fellow Masons at the expense of others in giving jobs, promotions, contracts and the like?*

A: Absolutely not. That would be a misuse of membership and subject to Masonic discipline. On his entry into Freemasonry each candidate states unequivocally that he expects no material gain from his membership. At various stages during the three ceremonies of his admission and when he is presented with a certificate from Grand Lodge that the admission ceremonies have been completed, he is forcefully reminded that attempts to gain preferment or material gain for himself or others is a misuse of membership which will not be tolerated. *The Book of Constitutions*, which every candidate receives, contains strict rules governing abuse of membership which can result in penalties varying from temporary suspension to expulsion.

Q: Isn't it true that Freemasons only look after each other?*

A: No. From its earliest days, Freemasonry has been involved in charitable activities. Since its inception, Freemasonry has provided support not only for widows and orphans of Freemasons but also for many others within the community. Whilst some Masonic charities cater specifically but not exclusively for Masons or their dependants, others make significant grants to non-Masonic organisations. On a local level, Lodges give substantial support to local causes.

Religion and politics

First and foremost, Freemasonry is not a religion. This is another of the most misunderstood areas of Freemasonry, often hampered by rumours spread by religious groups to discredit the Craft. Freemasonry is compatible with all religions and faiths and has a diverse membership of Christians, Jews, Muslims, Hindus, Sikhs and other denominations. There have been many religious leaders from all faiths that are or have been Freemasons, including archbishops, Orthodox priests, Muslim sheikhs, swamis and rabbis. There is a very useful book that discusses the subject of the compatibility of Freemasonry with Christianity (see *Workman Unashamed: The Testimony of a Christian Freemason* in the Further Information and Contacts section at the end of the book.) Here is a poem written by the famous Freemason and author, Rudyard Kipling, which beautifully illustrates the social, religious and racial diversity within a Lodge:

The Mother-Lodge

There was Rundle, Station Master,
  An' Beazeley of the Rail,
An' 'Ackman, Commissariat,
  An' Donkin' o' the Jail;
An' Blake, Conductor-Sargeant,
  Our Master twice was 'e,
With 'im that kept the Europe-shop,
  Old Framjee Eduljee.

Outside — "Sergeant! Sir! Salute! Salaam!"
Inside — "Brother", an' it doesn't do no 'arm.
We met upon the Level an' we parted on the Square,
An' I was Junior Deacon in my Mother-Lodge out there!

We'd Bola Nath, Accountant,
  An' Saul the Aden Jew,
An' Din Mohammed, draughtsman
  Of the Survey Office too;
There was Babu Chuckerbutty,
  An' Amir Singh the Sikh,
An' Castro from the fittin'-sheds,
  The Roman Catholick!
We 'adn't good regalia,
  An' our Lodge was old an' bare,
But we knew the Ancient Landmarks,
  An' we kep' 'em to a hair;
An' lookin' on it backwards
  It often strikes me thus,
There ain't such things as infidels,
  Excep', per'aps, it's us.

For monthly, after Labour,
  We'd all sit down and smoke
(We dursn't give no banquits,

Lest a Brother's caste were broke),
An' man on man got talkin'
Religion an' the rest,
An' every man comparin'
Of the God 'e knew the best.

So man on man got talkin',
An' not a Brother stirred
Till mornin' waked the parrots
An' that dam' brain-fever-bird;
We'd say 'twas 'ighly curious,
An' we'd all ride 'ome to bed,
With Mo'ammed, God, an' Shiva
Changin' pickets in our 'ead.

Full oft on Guv'ment service
This rovin' foot 'ath pressed,
An' bore fraternal greetin's
To the Lodges east an' west,
Accordin' as commanded
From Kohat to Singapore,
But I wish that I might see them
In my Mother-Lodge once more!
I wish that I might see them,
My Brethren black an' brown,
With the trichies smellin' pleasant
An' the hog-darn [cigar lighter] passin' down;
An' the old khansamah [butler] snorin'
On the bottle-khana [pantry] floor,
Like a Master in good standing
With my Mother-Lodge once more!

Outside — "Sergeant! Sir! Salute! Salaam!"
Inside — "Brother", an' it doesn't do no 'arm.
We met upon the Level an' we parted on the Square,
An' I was Junior Deacon in my Mother-Lodge out there!

Q: Aren't you a religion or a rival to religion?*

A: Emphatically not. Freemasonry requires a belief in God and its principles are common to many of the world's great religions. Freemasonry does not try to replace religion or substitute for it. Every candidate is exhorted to practise his religion and to regard its holy book as the unerring standard of truth. Freemasonry does not instruct its members in what their religious beliefs should be, nor does it offer sacraments. Freemasonry deals in relations between men; religion deals in a man's relationship with his god.

Q: What are all the strange symbols used in Freemasonry?

A: The symbols such as the well-known square and compasses are all items either used or mentioned in the rituals. There are many others, of which a few will be discussed in Chapter 2.

Q: Why do you have a Volume of the Sacred Law and not the Bible?*

A: To the majority of Freemasons the Volume of the Sacred Law is the Bible. There are many in Freemasonry, however, who are not Christian. To them the Bible is not their sacred book and they will make their promises on the book which is regarded as sacred to their religion. The Bible will always be present in an English lodge, but as the organisation welcomes men of many different faiths, it is called the Volume of the Sacred Law. Thus, when the Volume of the Sacred Law is referred to in ceremonies, to a non-Christian it will be the holy book of his religion and to a Christian it will be the Bible.

Q: Why do you call God the Great Architect?*

A: Freemasonry embraces all men who believe in God. Its membership includes Christians, Jews, Hindus, Sikhs, Muslims, Parsees and others. The use of descriptions such as the Great Architect prevents disharmony. The Great Architect is not a specific Masonic god or an attempt to combine all gods into one. Thus, men of differing religions pray together without offence being given to any of them.

Q: Why don't some churches like Freemasonry?*

A: There are elements within certain churches that misunderstand Freemasonry and confuse secular rituals with religious liturgy. Although the

Methodist Conference and the General Synod of the Anglican Church have occasionally criticised Freemasonry, in both churches there are many Masons and indeed others who are dismayed that the churches should attack Freemasonry, an organisation which has always encouraged its members to be active in their own religion.

Q: Why will Freemasonry not accept Roman Catholics as members?*
A: It does. The prime qualification for admission into Freemasonry has always been a belief in God. How that belief is expressed is entirely up to the individual. Four Grand Masters of English Freemasonry have been Roman Catholics. There are many Roman Catholic Freemasons.

Q: Isn't Freemasonry just another political pressure group?*
A: Emphatically not. Whilst individual Freemasons will have their own views on politics and state policy, Freemasonry as a body will never express a view on either. The discussion of politics at Masonic meetings has always been prohibited.

Q: Are there not Masonic Groups who are involved in politics?*
A: There are groups in other countries who call themselves Freemasons and who involve themselves in political matters. They are not recognised or countenanced by the United Grand Lodge of England and other regular Grand Lodges who follow the basic principles of Freemasonry and ban the discussion of politics and religion at their meetings.

Q: Is Freemasonry an international order?*
A: Only in the sense that Freemasonry exists throughout the free world. Each Grand Lodge is sovereign and independent, and whilst following the same basic principles, may have differing ways of passing them on. There is no international governing body for Freemasonry.

Q: How many Freemasons are there?*
A: Under the United Grand Lodge of England, there are 330,000 Freemasons, meeting in 8,644 Lodges. There are separate Grand Lodges for Ireland (north and south) and Scotland, with a combined membership of 150,000. Worldwide, there are probably 5 million members.

Q: What is the relationship between Freemasonry and groups like the Orange Order, Odd Fellows and Buffaloes?*
A: None. There are numerous fraternal orders and Friendly Societies whose rituals, regalia and organisation are similar in some respects to Freemasonry's. They have no formal or informal connections with Freemasonry.

Q: Why do you wear regalia?*
A: Wearing regalia is historical and symbolic and, like a uniform, serves to indicate to members where they rank in the organisation.

Q: Can a Mason be expelled?
A: Yes. If a Mason is convicted of a serious crime in a court of law or does anything to discredit the Craft, it is within his Lodge's rights and duty to expel him from Freemasonry.

Q: Who should be contacted if one wants to become a Freemason?*
A: In England and Wales, in addition to the Metropolitan Grand Lodge of London which has 1512 Lodges, there are 47 Masonic Provinces under the jurisdiction of the United Grand Lodge of England. These Provinces vary in respect to the number of Lodges they administer. They often correspond to the old county boundaries. If you don't know anyone at all who is a member, then get in touch with a Masonic Office (referred to as the Provincial Grand Lodge) in your area. Write to that office, telling them a little bit about yourself and your reasons for wishing to join. To find your local Provincial Grand Lodge, visit the UGLE website:
www.ugle.org.uk/provinces/lodges/hlodges.htm.
If you are in London, contact:

The Metropolitan Grand Lodge of London
33 Great Queen Street
London WC2B 5AA
Tel: 020 7539 2930

or

The Grand Secretary
The United Grand Lodge of England
Freemasons' Hall
60 Great Queen Street
London WC2B 5AZ
Tel: 020 7831 981

Arrangements will be made to meet you socially to find out more about you and to give you a chance to find out more about us. You would then in due course be invited to meet a committee of members from a Lodge you might be joining, prior to being balloted for membership of that Lodge. All being well, a date would then be fixed for your admission. If you are outside the UK: The United Grand Lodge of England has 730 Lodges operating in a number of countries around the world – please refer to the official UGLE website for more information: *www.ugle.org.uk/provinces/lodges/alodges.htm*

The United Grand Lodge of England runs a scheme to promote and encourage Freemasonry among undergraduates and other university members. If you are a current student or an alumnus of a university, you may well find that there is a specific Lodge associated with your institution. There are at present 15 Lodges participating in the Universities Scheme.

Some famous Freemasons

Monarchs
King George IV
King George VI
King Edward VII
King William IV
King Edward VIII
Frederick the Great, King of Prussia 1712-1786

Presidents/Statesmen
George Washington, US President
J. Edgar Hoover, First Director of the FBI
Franklin D. Roosevelt, US President
Theodore Roosevelt, US President
Gerald Ford, US President
Benjamin Franklin, Scientist and statesman
Emile Combes, French Prime Minister
Herbert Dunnico, Labour MP
Sir Winston Churchill, British Prime Minister
Bob Dole, US Senator

Actors/Entertainers
Jim Davidson, British comedian
Harry H. Corbett, actor, 'Steptoe and Son'
Harpo Marx – Marx Brothers
Bob Monkhouse – British comedian
Roy Rogers – American singer and cowboy actor
Harry Houdini – magician and escapologist
Mel Blanc – voice of cartoon characters Bugs Bunny and Daffy Duck
Oliver Hardy – American actor, (Laurel & Hardy)
Cecil B. De Mille – American film-maker
Douglas Fairbanks, Snr. – An American actor
Harold C. Lloyd – American silent movie actor
Richard Pryor – American actor and comedian

Clark Gable – American actor
Peter Sellers – British actor
Roger de Courcey – British comedian and ventriloquist

Writers/Poets/Artists
Mark Twain – American author
Oscar Wilde – Irish playwright, novelist and poet
William Hogarth – English painter
Sir P. G. Wodehouse – English author
Alexander Pope – English poet
Robert Burns – Scottish poet
Sir Walter Scott – Scottish novelist and poet
William Blake – English poet and painter
Sir Arthur Conan Doyle – Scottish author
Rudyard Kipling – English author

Composers/Musicians
Wolfgang Amadeus Mozart – composer
Franz Joseph Haydn – composer
Franz Liszt – composer
Sir W. S. Gilbert – librettist (Gilbert & Sullivan)
Sir Arthur Sullivan – composer (Gilbert & Sullivan)
Irving Berlin – composer
Louis Armstrong – jazz musician
Nat 'King' Cole – American pianist and singer

Religious Leaders
Dr Geoffrey Fisher – Archbishop of Canterbury (1945-61)
Sultan Sir Mohamed Shah – third Aga Khan and spiritual leader
Rev Norman Vincent Peale – Methodist Minister and author
Sir Israel Brodie – Chief Rabbi, United Kingdom (1945-65)
Joseph Smith – founder of the Mormon Church
Abd El-Kader – Muslim leader and Sufi
Swami Yogi Vivekananda – philosopher and theologian

Other notable Freemasons
Edward Jenner – English physician, discovered a vaccine for smallpox
Sir Christopher Wren – English architect of St Paul's Cathedral
Buzz Aldrin – American astronaut and second man on the Moon
John 'Jackie' Milburn – English footballer
William H. 'Jack' Dempsey – American boxer
Sir Malcolm Campbell – English motor racer and journalist
Sir Donald Campbell – British car and motorboat racer

2

The Craft

Freemasons' Hall, London

Now that your husband is a Freemason, what is he going to be doing?

In this chapter we will give you a brief history of Freemasonry and a simple explanation of the three Craft degrees, what they involve and what they mean to a Freemason.

Craft or 'Regular' Freemasonry (known as Blue Lodge Masonry in the United States) applies to all Freemasonry under the jurisdiction of the United Grand Lodge of England which follows the rituals of the Three Degrees. There are many other branches of Freemasonry around the world which come under the jurisdiction of their own Grand Lodges. We will discuss this briefly later in the chapter, but for now we will give an explanation of Craft Freemasonry.

Q: How and where did Freemasonry start?*
A: It is not known. The earliest recorded 'making' of a Freemason in England is that of Elias Ashmole in 1646. Organised Freemasonry began with the founding of the Grand Lodge of England on 24 June 1717, the first Grand Lodge in the

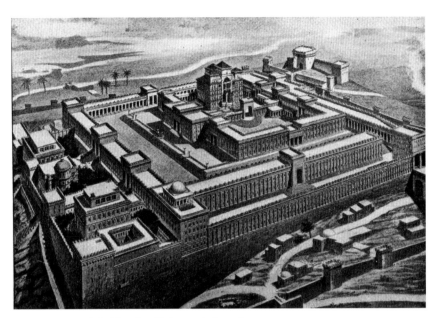

Reconstruction of the Temple of Solomon in Jerusalem

world. Ireland followed in 1725 and Scotland in 1736. All the regular Grand Lodges in the world trace themselves back to one or more of the Grand Lodges in the British Isles. There are two main theories of origin. According to one, the operative stonemasons who built the great cathedrals and castles had lodges in which they discussed trade affairs. They had simple initiation ceremonies and, as there were no City and Guilds certificates, dues cards or trade union membership cards, they adopted secret signs and words to demonstrate that they were trained masons when they moved from site to site. In the 1600s, these operative lodges began to accept non-operatives as 'gentlemen masons'. Gradually these non-operatives took over the lodges and turned them from operative to 'free and accepted' or 'speculative' lodges.

The other theory is that in the late 1500s and early 1600s, there was a group which was interested in the promotion of religious and political tolerance in an age of great intolerance when differences of opinion on matters of religion and politics were to lead to bloody civil war. In forming Freemasonry, they were trying to make better men and build a better world. As the means of teaching in those days was by allegory and symbolism, they took the idea of building as the central allegory on which to form their system. The main source of allegory was the Bible, the contents of which were known to everyone even if they could not read, and the only building described in detail in the Bible was King Solomon's Temple, which became the basis of the ritual. The old trade guilds provided them with their basis administration of a Master, Wardens, Treasurer and Secretary, and the operative mason's tools provided them with a wealth of symbols with which to illustrate the moral teachings of Freemasonry.

Q: How many degrees are there in Freemasonry?
A: Basic Freemasonry consists of the three Craft degrees:
• Entered Apprentice
• Fellow Craft and
• Master Mason.

This can be then followed by the Royal Arch degree, known as Chapter. There are many other Masonic degrees and orders which are called 'additional' because they add to the basis of the Craft and Royal Arch. They are not basic to Freemasonry but add to it by further expounding and illustrating the principles stated in the Craft and Royal Arch. Some of these additional degrees are numerically superior to the Third Degree, but this does not affect the fact that they are additional to and not in anyway superior to or higher than the Craft. The ranks that these additional degrees carry have no standing with the Craft or Royal Arch.

Q: What do Freemasons wear in Lodge?
A: Freemasons are required to wear a simple dark suit, black tie or Grand Lodge tie, white gloves and the regalia (apron etc) of their rank. See above.

Q: Isn't ritual out of place in a modern society?*
A: No. The ritual is a shared experience which binds the members together. Its use of drama, allegory and symbolism impresses the principles and teachings more firmly in the mind of each candidate than if they were simply passed on to him in matter-of-fact modern language.

Q: Why do grown men run around with their trousers rolled up?*
A: It is true that candidates have to roll up their trouser legs during the three ceremonies when they are being admitted to membership. Taken out of context, this can seem amusing, but like many other aspects of Freemasonry, it has a symbolic meaning.

Q: Why do Masons wear white gloves?
A: The gloves worn by the candidate are intended to teach him that the acts of a Mason should be as pure and spotless as the gloves he now wears (not that they stay very white unless we remind them to give them a good wash every so often!)

White gloves

There is an interesting quote describing a custom in European Freemasonry from an old text called *The Symbolism of Freemasonry. Illustrating and explaining its Science and Philosophy, its Legends, Myths, and Symbols.*

"In the continental rites of Masonry, as practised in France, in Germany, and in other countries of Europe, it is an invariable custom to present the newly-initiated candidate not only, as we do, with a white leather apron, but also with two pairs of white kid gloves, one a man's pair for himself, and the other a woman's, to be presented by him in turn to his wife or his betrothed, according to the custom of the German masons, or, according to the French, to the female whom he most esteems, 'which, indeed, amounts, or should amount, to the same thing'."
— *Albert G. Mackey, MD, Edition 1882*

Q: What happens at a Lodge Meeting?*
A: The meeting is in two parts. As in any association there is a certain amount of administrative procedure: minutes of the last meeting, proposing and balloting for new members, discussing and voting on financial matters, election of officers, news and correspondence. Then there are the ceremonies for admitting new Masons and the annual installation of the Master and appointment of officers. The three ceremonies for admitting a new Mason are in two parts: a slight dramatic instruction in the principles and lessons taught

A Meeting of Freemasons for the Admission of Masters, by Thomas Palser, London, 1812

in the Craft followed by a lecture in which the candidate's various duties are spelled out.

Q: What are the Three Degrees?
A: Freemasonry in its teachings could be described as the story of life. Its wisdom represents the progression of life for a man, demonstrated in allegory and symbolism through three moral plays performed in the Lodge.

The First Degree – Initiation
The First Degree symbolises birth: coming from darkness and ignorance to light. It is the basics of being a good and moral man. The candidate is blindfolded, his foot slipshod and a noose placed around his neck. He is led into the Masonic Lodge room assisted by those more experienced than him and takes part in a ritual that teaches him never to reveal the secrets of Masonry to anyone. He is taught that he is expected to be a good man and never to rush into things blindly, but also never to back off from the challenges of life. He is instructed to create balance, dividing his time wisely during each

Entered Apprentice apron

day of his life and to keep all vain and unbecoming thoughts under control. He is also taught never to turn his back on someone who needs his help. When he has taken the solemn vow to become a Mason his blindfold is taken off and he is restored to the light. He is now an Entered Apprentice Mason. The regalia worn by the Entered Apprentice is a simple white leather apron.

The Second Degree – Passing

The Second Degree symbolises life and the lessons the Mason must learn to find the answers to the knowledge he seeks. The candidate is encouraged to learn, to work hard, to assist others and to contribute to charity. The lesson is about hopes and ambitions but with the willingness to labour for rewards. Once he has passed through the Second Degree, the Entered Apprentice becomes a Fellow Craft Mason. The regalia worn by the Fellow Craft is a white apron with two blue rosettes.

Fellow Craft apron

The Third Degree – Raising

The Third Degree symbolises death and our need to face this inevitability. Freemasonry can give the candidate confidence to face death in the light of promised resurrection and in doing so he understands that he must symbolically die before he can be reborn. The Fellow Craft has now earned the title of Master Mason. The regalia worn by the Master Mason is a white apron with three blue rosettes.

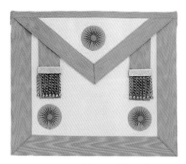

Master Mason's apron

Below is a beautiful verse describing how a newly made Master Mason felt after he went through his Third Degree.

Last Night I Knelt Where Hiram Knelt

Last night I knelt where Hiram knelt
and took an obligation.
Today I'm closer to my God
for I'm a Master Mason.
Though heretofore my fellow men
seemed each one like the other,
Today I search each one apart.
I'm looking for my Brother.
And as I feel his friendly grip
it fills my heart with pride.
I know while I am on the square
that he is by my side.
His footsteps on my errand go
if I should such require.
His prayers will lead in my behalf
if I should so desire.
My words are safe within his breast
as though within my own,
His hand forever at my back
to help me safely home.
Good counsel whispers in my ear
and warns of any danger.
By square and compass, Brother now
who once would call me stranger.
I might have lived a moral life
and risen to distinction
Without my Brother's helping hand
and the fellowship of Masons.
But God, who knows how hard it is
to resist life's temptations,
Knows why I knelt where Hiram knelt
and took that obligation.

— *Author unknown*

Festive Board - Freemasons' Hall London. Reproduced by kind permission of the Grand Lodge of British Columbia and Yukon.

Q: What happens after the ceremony?
A: The Festive Board is held, which involves a dinner, toasts, speeches and a collection for charity.

After the Three Degrees
Once your husband has completed his Three Degrees and become a Master Mason, he has the opportunity to join other Lodges. These are generally referred to as 'side orders' and are numerous and varied, all involving different rituals and regalia. These orders (except Royal Arch) are not part of 'regular' Freemasonry under the jurisdiction of the United Grand Lodge of England and the Mason should remain within his Craft Lodge.

The temptation is often to join as many as possible, but the Mason must always consider his commitment to his family, work and financial status before leaping in. The list of side orders is extensive, but we will mention a few more well known ones.

Royal Arch – Royal Arch is described as the continuation of Craft Freemasonry and the completion of "pure, ancient Masonry". It continues the lessons learnt in the Three Degrees to a new level of contemplation of man's spiritual nature.

Royal Arch apron and sash

Order of Mark Master Masons – in England, Europe and Australasia this order confers the Mark Degree which is similar to Craft Freemasonry in that it uses the ritualised allegory of the building of King Solomon's Temple. Its governing body is The Grand Lodge of Mark Master Masons of England and Wales and its Districts and Lodges Overseas which also controls the Royal Ark Mariner degree, conferred in separately warranted Royal Ark Mariner Lodges.

The Ancient and Accepted (Scottish) Rite – also known as Scottish Rite or Rose Croix. From Master Mason, this order confers a further 29 degrees, totalling 33.

Knights Templar (KT) – This international philanthropic Order is open to all Masons of Christian faith (this varies from jurisdiction to jurisdiction).

The Symbolism of Freemasonry

Q: What do the square and compasses and other symbols mean?
A: There are many symbols used in Freemasonry and unless you understand a bit about them it can seem a bit confusing and strange. Below are depictions and meanings of the most commonly seen symbols. Bear in mind that symbolism can be interpreted differently by each of us as individuals. The meanings given here are not meant to be exclusively definitive.

Freemasonry has been described as "A Peculiar system of Morality, Veiled in Allegory and Illustrated with Symbols". This was written several hundred years ago and may seem a bit strange, but if we break it down it becomes quite simple.

A Peculiar system of Morality – the word 'peculiar' used to mean 'special' or 'unique', whereas today we know it to mean 'strange' or 'unusual'. So really it means 'a special/unique system of Morality'.

Veiled in Allegory – this is a bit trickier. Allegory means 'the representation of abstract ideas or principles by characters, figures, or events in narrative, dramatic or pictorial form' – so essentially it means that there is more than one possible interpretation and that the meaning(s) are hidden.

Illustrated with Symbols – the symbols therefore are illustrative of the morality and allegory of Freemasonry.

So a more modern interpretation would be 'A unique way of teaching men about morality using special plays and visual aids!' The most commonly seen symbols:

Square and Compasses

The set square and compasses represent the primary working tools of a mason: the compasses to create a perfect circle and the square to check accuracy of measurements. Symbolically the square represents the moral law, the law by which the Mason rules his life, and the compasses represent power of judgement and the ability to see one's limits. Together they represent the aim of Freemasonry which is to match one's personal judgement with the moral law.

The Letter 'G'

This symbol has many meanings to different Freemasons and indeed different Lodges, so it can represent:
- God or a Supreme Being
- Geometry – the basis of the work of the stonemasons from which Freemasonry may have originated
- Goodness – the essential goodness inherent in Freemasonry and mankind
- Or even an ancient Scots word 'greegriment' – meaning 'harmony'.

The Broken Column

The broken column symbolises the death of the
Master Mason and architect Hiram Abiff before his
work was completed on King Solomon's Temple.
    The symbol was first used as a brooch for the wives
and sweethearts of Masons during the American Civil
War. As many of the men didn't return home, it was soon adopted as a
symbol of Masonic widows. Today it is still given to the widow of a
Freemason, so that she may be identified as such and given the courtesies she
is due along with any assistance she is entitled to (see Chapter 6).

The All-Seeing Eye

The All-Seeing Eye is a symbol of the Omnipresent
Deity. King Solomon alludes to this in the *Book of*
Proverbs 15:3: "The eyes of the Lord are in every place,
beholding [keeping watch upon] the evil and the good."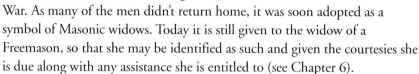

The Skull and Crossbones

The skull and crossbones are an important emblem in Masonry,
symbolising the transience of the material world, and are
used in initiation rituals as a symbol of rebirth. It was
also traditionally used in *memento mori* [Latin:
remember that you have to die] which were illustrative
reminders of our mortality. This in turn reminds all
Masons to do good while they are alive.

The Acacia leaf

This delightful little leaf holds a deep meaning, that of
the immortality of the soul. This is because the acacia
tree has the ability to regrow from just a tiny cutting
and so symbolises death and rebirth. In ancient times
sprigs of acacia were traditionally placed upon the
newly dug grave at funerals, to show that as the
evergreen renews itself, so does the soul. The following
passage is from an old Masonic funeral service, sadly no longer used:

"This evergreen is an emblem of our faith in the immortality of the soul. By this we are reminded that we have an immortal part within us, which shall survive the grave, and which shall never, never, never die."

The Forget-me-not

As mentioned in Chapter 1, this is a symbol often worn by modern Masons as a sign of respect for those persecuted for being Freemasons during the Nazi regime and World War 2. It was originally worn by the German Freemasons to discreetly display their membership (the square and compasses would have been too dangerous to wear or display) and also by the Masonic prisoners of war held in concentration camps to signify that the light of Freemasonry would not be extinguished.

The Three Graces and the Cardinal Virtues

Faith, Hope and Charity. Frontispiece: *An Encyclopedia of Freemasonry and its Kindred Sciences.* Albert G. Mackey, Masonic History Company, New York 1917

Don't worry if you hear Faith, Hope, Charity, Temperance, Prudence, Fortitude and Justice mentioned, they are not a group of females encountered whilst your husband is out at Lodge, they are in fact qualities and virtues Freemasons hope to emulate!

Faith, Hope and Charity

"Freemasonry aims at the promotion of all that is pure and good and noble in human character, and therefore its lessons and symbols are much devoted to the inculcation of faith, hope and charity, in which the excellence of human character mainly consists. However men may differ in their religious beliefs, no one who holds the primary doctrines can hold any doubt that faith, hope and charity are the three great religious graces on which the whole character and conduct of a man depends."
— *Freemasonry: The Three Masonic Graces, Faith, Hope and Charity.* Chalmers I. Paton (1878)

Temperance, Prudence, Fortitude and Justice

Four Cardinal Virtues – Temperance, Prudence, Fortitude and Justice. Frontispiece: *An Encyclopedia of Freemasonry and its Kindred Sciences Vol. II.* Albert G. Mackey, Masonic History Company, New York 1917

Temperance – the trait of avoiding excesses
Prudence – discretion in practical affairs
Fortitude – strength of mind that enables one to endure adversity with courage
Justice – conformity to moral rightness in action or attitude; righteousness.

And finally…

Q: Am I allowed to buy my husband Masonic gifts?
A: Absolutely! There are many excellent suppliers selling books, pin badges, gloves, wallets, diaries and other useful gifts and they would be more than happy to recommend something if you are unsure of what to buy – see Masonic Suppliers at the end of the book.

Masonic humour

There's a man walking back from his Lodge meeting at one o'clock in the morning and he's very drunk. A policeman stops him and asks, "Where are you going in that condition?" Man: "Iimm on mmyy waayyy to a lectttuurre on Ffreemmassonnrrry." Officer: "Where can you possibly get a lecture on Freemasonry at this time of night?" Man: "Frromm mmyy wifffe, wwhenn I gget homme!"

3

From Entered Apprentice to Worshipful Master

This chapter describes the offices (jobs) relating to mainstream Craft Freemasonry, (also known as 'Blue Lodge Freemasonry' in the United States). Every Masonic Lodge appoints Lodge officers to carry various jobs within the Lodge.

Each year the Worshipful Master decides on who will take position of each office, each Brother taking on a progressive position until he reaches the point where he is Worshipful Master himself. The role the new Mason will take is usually that of Steward and he will progress through the junior offices to the principal offices in the following order:

Progressive officers
- Steward
- Inner Guard
- Junior Deacon
- Senior Deacon
- Junior Warden
- Senior Warden
- Worshipful Master (WM)

Steward
It is usual for newly made Masons to fill this junior office supervised by a more senior member, often a Past Master. Their duties may include the following:

- Stewards have a traditional role of setting up the place-cards before dinner and serving drinks during the Festive Board.

Steward emblem

- They may be required to understudy the position of the Senior or Junior Deacons in their absence.
- During a degree ceremony, a Steward (or more) may be required to assist the Deacons in conducting the candidates around the Temple.

Inner Guard

The office of Inner Guard is usually given to a fairly junior member and provides an opportunity for him to observe ceremonies and display his own abilities.

The Inner Guard shares the task of guarding the Temple door with the Tyler. However, as the name suggests, the Inner Guard is on the inside of the door, whilst the Tyler remains outside. He is often armed with a short dagger called a poignard.

Inner Guard emblem

Junior Deacon and Senior Deacon

The Deacon's role is to guide the candidates during the ceremonies. Both roles as Deacons are very rewarding and interesting, as it is a perfect opportunity to learn ritual whilst making the ceremony an enjoyable and caring experience for the candidates.

In Craft Lodges the symbol of the Deacons is a dove and is depicted on badges of office. It is also in sculpted form on the top of the ceremonial wands commonly carried by Deacons. However, in the United States, the Junior Deacon's badge is a crescent moon in the centre of the square and compass, and the Senior Deacon's is a blazing sun upon a square and compass.

Deacon emblem

Junior Warden emblem

Junior and Senior Wardens

The Wardens have differing but complementary roles within the Lodge. They assist the Worshipful Master in opening and closing the Lodge and the Junior Warden works with the Inner Guard to ensure that unqualified men do not enter the Temple.

The Junior Warden's symbol is a plumb-rule, a stonemason's

tool for measuring the accuracy of vertical alignment. The symbol of the Senior Warden is the level, a stonemason's tool for measuring the accuracy of horizontal alignment.

Senior Warden emblem

Worshipful Master

The office of Worshipful Master is the highest honour, other than initiation, to which a Lodge may appoint any of its members. The Worshipful Master is elected, generally by means of a secret ballot. However, in most Lodges the position will almost always be filled by the previous year's Senior Warden. The Worshipful Master sits in the East of the Lodge room and directs all the business of the Lodge. He also presides over the rituals and ceremonies.

Now that your husband is 'in the Chair', he will have quite a full year, as not only does he need to know his ritual off by heart (this is where your help will be invaluable!) but he also has to make various decisions concerning the Lodge. He will need to be a master of many roles – diplomat, friend, advisor, critic and upholder of all that Freemasonry stands for. He will need to attend rehearsal of ritual, as pride in an efficient and moving ceremony is of great importance. Be prepared to help him with his ritual learning, for not only is it a wonderful insight into his Masonic work but it will be eternally appreciated! You may become slightly tired of seeing the 'little blue book', but it is a great honour to be asked to help.

Handbooks are available for all the offices mentioned and are invaluable for guiding through each step in the Masonic journey. These can make a really useful gift for your husband. (See the Recommended Reading section at the end of the book).

Worshipful Master emblem

4

Ladies' Night and Charity Do's

So he has finally made it to the Chair and is now Master of the Lodge. What does this mean for you as the Master's Lady?

Some Ladies do not wish to get involved in their partner's year as Master, but those who do can enjoy a rewarding and memorable year. Being elected as Master of the Lodge is the greatest honour that a Lodge can bestow on any member and as such both the Master and his Lady are treated with the utmost respect and regard by the other members. You may be asked by other Lodges within the area to attend their functions as representatives of your partner's Lodge and your circle of friends and acquaintances may grow over the year. Some Lodges do not encourage active participation by the ladies but the trend nowadays seems to be that most Lodges like to encourage occasions where the ladies can join them. Depending on the type of Lodge that your partner is a member of, you could help them to move forward and encourage them to include the ladies a little more or you could continue the traditions already in place.

In the United States, the wives and families of Masons tend to socialise a lot more, organising barbecues, charity events and even home groups. This has led to the formation of the *Masonic Wives' Association*, which does charitable work and also visits other wives who have given birth, sick Masons (or their wives) and the widows of deceased Masons, usually taking with them a gift or a 'purse' of money. In Delhi, India, the wives have embraced this concept and established the *All India Association of Mason's Wives*. Their objective is "to do good, meaningful and worthwhile service" and to make the order "a platform for improvement and enrichment of our own lives and more importantly the lives of the less fortunate of our society." As you can see, starting your own ladies' group is a perfect way to become more involved in Lodge life and also a very worthwhile way to raise money for local, national or international causes.

So where to start and how can you make a difference?

A good place to start would be on the night of your partner's installation. You could send out an invitation to the partners of the other Brethren, asking them to join you for an informal dinner. This might be held somewhere else in the Lodge rooms (many buildings have several rooms) or, if this is not possible, at a nearby hotel or restaurant. At this dinner you could introduce yourself to those who do not know you and welcome them to the wider family of the Lodge and also introduce them to other ladies present. It can be very daunting for the partner of a new Mason and an informal invitation like this where they could be taken under your wing will help them feel at ease and so enjoy functions in the future, knowing you will be there as a friendly face. During the course of the evening you could discuss ideas you may have for other social events during the year and find out what the other ladies would find enjoyable. You might suggest meeting regularly when the men are at the Lodge as many ladies do, thus enhancing their own social lives rather than becoming 'Masonic widows'. Some ladies will welcome these opportunities, but there will always be those who are reluctant to join in. That is fine, but do always invite them to anything you arrange as they may change their minds.

The Master and his Lady usually decide on a charity that has special meaning to them to support in some way during their year. You might also tell the ladies about any charity that you have chosen and the reasons why you have chosen it. You could ask them to support you: a plastic milk container with a slit cut in the top holds quite a few coppers and you could ask them to help you collect a 'pint of pennies'. This is a fun way to raise a bit of money and getting the other ladies on board this way makes them feel that you want them to be involved without feeling any pressure. Hopefully by the end of the evening new friendships will have been made and you will all be looking forward to the next time you get together.

There are many different types of functions which you can arrange during the year depending on the kind of people involved with the Lodge. What is right for one Lodge will not necessarily work for another. Find out what functions have been popular in the past and maybe try and introduce something different as well. We have attended Sunday lunches, quizzes, skittles evenings, barn dances, cabarets and barbecues, to name but a few. It is a good idea to have some functions where the whole family can attend. Masons with younger families welcome social events where the children are welcome; it saves having to worry about babysitters and the children enjoy the attention which they receive from the Brethren and the ladies present.

Whatever you decide to do, being well organised is the key to a successful event. Your partner will probably enlist the help of another member of the Lodge to assist with the organisation of the event such as sending out letters and collecting money, but it is important that you keep fully involved. Remember, these events are social functions and whilst the men still like to keep up their formalities, it is up to you as the Lady to welcome people and make them feel at ease.

Once you have decided on the type of function you are going to hold and suitable bookings have been provisionally made, a letter should be sent to all Lodge members. As we mentioned before, in some areas invitations are also sent to the Masters of other local Lodges if appropriate. The letter will be from the Master and his Lady and should be informative but not too formal. It should be sent out in plenty of time to give people the best possible chance of being able to attend, as many Masons are very busy and their diaries tend to fill up quickly. Make it clear in the letter what type of function it is that you are holding, whether children are welcome, non-Masonic guests can be invited, etc. It is also a good idea to give advice on the dress code for the event as for many ladies attending Masonic functions the "what should I wear?" dilemma can be the most daunting of all. There is nothing worse than arriving at a function feeling either under- or over-dressed. Just an indication in the letter stating a dress code of casual, formal, informal or evening dress for events such as Ladies' Night will help. Most ladies will be grateful for this clue – it's all right for the men and they just don't understand!

The letter should also give a date by which you would like a reply and/or money so that you can make any necessary adjustments to the plans you may have provisionally made and so that firm bookings can be made. You will quite often seek the help of another Lodge member to assist with the collecting of money and as a point of contact for correspondence. Ladies' evenings normally have an official Festival Secretary appointed. This will be covered in more detail later in the chapter.

Once everything is in place for the planned function you can think about how you might raise some money for your chosen charity and arrange prizes for raffles or for any other ideas that you may have. Below are a few fundraising ideas that we have come across over the years which may be of interest to you.

A 10p auction

This kind of auction is quite good fun and a lot of money can be raised without anyone feeling as if they have spent a fortune.

You will need one item of reasonable value, such as a bottle of spirits. The bid starts off at 10p and each subsequent bid increases by 10p. The secret to the success of this auction is that each bid is actually paid for at the time it is placed. In other words, you bid 10p, put 10p in the bin, the next person bids 20p and puts their 20p in the bin and so on. You continue in this way until no more bids are made. You will be amazed by the amount of money you have raised. An item selling for a final bid of £5 will actually have raised the staggering sum of £127.50, so as you can see this is a very worthwhile type of auction.

Heads or tails

This is a very simple way of raising money. All stand in the centre of the room with a £1 coin in their hand. Each person tosses their coin and covers it on the back of their hand. The caller (you or someone on your behalf) tosses their coin and shouts out the result, 'heads' or 'tails'. Everyone who has the same as the caller puts their coin into the bin and sits down. Everyone who remains standing repeats the process until there is an eventual winner. You will have raised some money and everyone will have had some fun.

Sit down raffle or bingo

Everyone buys a ticket and the numbers are pulled out of a hat. If your number is called you sit down. Last one standing wins the prize. Whatever you decide to do, being well organised and having fun are the most important things. Fundraising, whilst important, should normally only be a small part of the whole event.

The function will normally end with the Master thanking everyone for attending, If a fundraising event has taken place then it is important to advise everyone how much has been raised and thank people for their generosity. It may be at this point that you give details of any other functions that are planned as people are often quite receptive to future ideas when they have just experienced a good evening out.

Ladies' Night

The main social event of the Master's year will be the Ladies' Night which is held in honour of his Lady and the ladies of other members of the Lodge. This is usually a grand affair calling for black tie for the gentlemen and evening dress for the ladies. It is a wonderful celebration of the ladies and the whole evening is aimed at making them feel special.

A brief history of the Ladies' Night

The exact date of the first Ladies' Night is not known, but records do show some occurring in the late 1700s. However, by the 19th century, annual festivals and balls, to which ladies and non-Masons were invited, were regularly held by Lodges. Although not classed specifically as 'Ladies' Nights' it would seem from records of the speeches from these events that these occasions were held deliberately to thank the ladies for their support.

By the early 20th century, we have evidence of elaborate programmes produced to celebrate 'Ladies' Night'. These were often beautifully produced with gold embossing, delicate illustrations and additional decorations such as tassels or miniature pencils attached. The menus varied from decade to decade – the late Victorian/early Edwardian menus showed sumptuous dishes made up of many courses. As the years went by, fashions changed and by the 1940s, the menus reflected the wartime rationing and included soup, some chicken and vegetables and a very simple rice pudding. Gifts for the ladies ranged from jewellery, perfume bottles and pill boxes to glove stretchers. There was usually music and dancing and often a whist drive, but it is evident from the programmes that it truly was a special night and every effort was made to make the ladies feel very appreciated and loved. Here are a few quotes from some vintage programmes:

"To greet you on this festive night
Is our pleasure, pride and duty.
What more can add to our delight
Than your presence, grace and beauty."

*****

"To make you happy is our care
A really delightful time to share!"

*****

"Married couples resemble a pair of shears, so joined that they cannot be separated. Often moving in opposite directions, yet always punishing anyone who comes between them."

*****

Organising your Ladies' Night

A point worth mentioning here is the cost of Ladies' Night, as this can be a cause for concern, though does not have to be the case. A well-planned evening can be covered by the cost of the tickets without this being too high. Years ago, in some cases, young Masons were advised to take out a savings plan to help them pay for Ladies' Night: this is no longer necessary. Careful negotiation with most hotels can result in room charges being waived. They will not offer this, but most will agree with some persuasion when they realise the amount of business you will bring to the venue on the evening. Often guests book rooms and usually plenty is spent over the bar!

Planning in advance to source ladies' gifts ensures that you can secure good deals: if you leave it till the week before you will panic buy. Even booking the band and hotel early can save you money. Book up to 12 months in advance and you may pay last year's prices and they will always be more receptive to negotiations when the diary is looking empty. Meals need not be as lavish as they used to be. Most people will be satisfied with three or four courses. Again, negotiate for better deals.

You may wish to look at the website Ladies' Festivals for some helpful tips. The address is *www.ladiesfestivals.net*

The higher the number of guests, the cheaper you make the tickets. A typical example is given below. Remember, this is only a guideline, but it will give you some idea of what costs might be involved. For example sundry costs to cover the cost of:

Band	£500
Flowers	£200
Printing	£50
Other gifts	£50

Total: £800 (these costs to be divided by the expected number of guests; e.g. 100 guests, a cost of £8 per ticket). To this add the cost of the meal and half of the cost of the ladies' gift (presuming your guests will be roughly half male and half female)

So for example:

Meal	£20
Ladies' gift	£2.50 (half of the £5 cost)
Sundries	£8
Ticket price	£30.50

In this example all of the costs would be covered. Depending on your individual circumstances you may subsidise the costs if you wish.

We heard of one Mason who was fast approaching the Chair and was so worried about the costs of Ladies' Night that he was considering dropping out of his Lodge rather than face the embarrassment of being unable to fund the evening. His concerns were mentioned to us and after seeing the above example he decided to go ahead. After careful planning and negotiation, he hosted a very successful evening. It can be done!

The organisation of Ladies' Night needs lots of planning and a Festival Secretary is normally appointed to work alongside the Master and his Lady to ensure the smooth running of the evening. A venue which is suitable for a large party is needed and either the Masonic hall or a local hotel should be booked for the occasion. Entertainment is usually some kind of band or disco; remember, you have to cater for a wide range of ages so a live band is generally more favourable. Invitations are sent out and Brethren are encouraged to invite their non-Masonic friends as well as members of other Lodges.

Once you have an idea of numbers then the question of ladies' gifts is usually discussed. The ladies' gift is just a token given to each lady as a memento of the evening. Gifts vary so much from Lodge to Lodge that it is impossible to say what should be given if indeed anything at all. Many Lodges in more recent years have decided not to give a ladies' gift but to make a donation to charity instead. A good idea that may be useful is to visit the website of a charity that you would like to support and see if there are any suitable gifts there which could be used. This way the lady gets a token of the evening and is doubly rewarded by knowing that the money paid for the gift is also supporting a very worthwhile cause. A good example of this is Breast Cancer Awareness, that does a lovely range of lapel pins at varying prices and works for a cause which many women would be happy to support. Whatever is decided about the gift, this should not be a burden on the Master and his Lady, but something that they are both comfortable with.

The next thing that needs to be organised is the table plan. As Ladies' Night is a formal occasion there is usually a top table and then either legs or round tables depending on the room and the preferences of the Master and his Lady. Table decorations need to be arranged or at least discussed with the venue provider as does a colour theme. The Festival Secretary will assist with all of this and arrange for any printing that you may want such as name place-cards and menu cards. There are outlets for purchasing the stationery needed, but with the improvement in computers and the skill of the people using them, many Festival Secretaries, or someone else in the Lodge, are able to produce some unique designs that are equally acceptable. A nice touch on the menu card is to include some suitable quotes. We give below a few ideas of quotes which may be used.

"You don't love a woman because she is beautiful, but she is beautiful because you love her!" *Anonymous*

"True friendship is like sound health: the value of it is seldom known until it is lost." *Charles Caleb Colton*

"A wife laughs at her husband's jokes, not because they are clever, but because she is." *Unknown*

"Love is blind, friendship closes its eyes." *Proverb*

"A lady's imagination is very rapid, it jumps from admiration to love, from love to matrimony in a moment." *Jane Austen, Pride and Prejudice*

"There is only one happiness in life: to love and be loved." *George Sand*

"Behind every successful woman – is herself!" *Anonymous*

"I get by with a little help from my friends." *John Lennon*

"A friend is a gift you give yourself." *Robert Louis Stevenson*

"Coffee, chocolate, MEN – some things are just better rich!" *Unknown*

"I count myself in nothing else so happy, as in a soul rememb'ring my good friends." *William Shakespeare*

"Kind words are short and easy to speak, but their echoes are truly endless." *Mother Theresa*

"A woman is like a tea bag … You don't know how strong she is until you put her in hot water!" *Anonymous*

There are, of course, many, many more quotes; these are just some of our favourites.

Quite often the menu card is passed around to the guests during the course of the evening and they all sign it for the Master and his Lady to have a permanent record of those who attended the function. This is lovely to look back on years later and evokes many fond memories of an enjoyable evening.

Once everything is in place and all of the arrangements are confirmed the Festival Secretary will liaise with the Director of Ceremonies as to how the event is going to run so that the Master and his Lady have an enjoyable evening without any stress apart from making speeches that is but we will come to that later.

The evening usually starts quite early with a reception at which all of the guests are presented to the Master and his Lady by the Director of Ceremonies. Quite often a photographer is present and each set of guests has their photograph taken either on their own or with the Master and his Lady or sometimes both. This is normally followed by a banquet. Once everyone is seated the Master and his Lady are announced and enter the room escorted by the Director of Ceremonies to the clapping of their guests. The walk from the entrance to your place at the top table can seem like a marathon when all the attention is on you! There then follows a formal dinner and it is the usual practice for the Wardens and the Master of the Lodge to use their gavels as they would at their normal Festive Boards to attract the attention of the guests for such things as grace, wine takings and toasts. Wine taking is a personal decision, but if anyone is not sure what to do then a usual format would perhaps be as follows:

- The Master takes wine with his Lady
- The Master takes wine with all of the ladies (he may wish to say that they may remain seated)
- The Lady takes wine with all of the gentlemen (she may state that they should stand!)
- The Master and his Lady may take wine with their personal guests
- They may wish to take wine with guests who have the same interests as they do, i.e. all Boy Scouts/Girl Guides, all fishermen, thespians, etc
- Sometimes the Master will take wine with the other Freemasons in the room or more specifically members of his Lodge
- The Master may wish to take wine with his Wardens, or in some cases the Master and his Lady may take wine with the Wardens and their ladies
- The Master usually takes wine with his Festival Secretary.

All of these wine takings are given as suggestions which you may wish to use. In all cases it is best to time wine takings to suit the progress of the meal, perhaps as a course is coming to an end rather than as it is being served. The Director of Ceremonies will oversee all matters at the Festive Board and will normally be experienced at running this type of event.

Once the meal has finished there is normally a short comfort break and once everyone is reseated the toasts for the evening will commence. (The toast to the Queen may take place before the break.) The main toast of the evening will be the toast to the ladies. A member of the Lodge will have been asked in advance to prepare a short toast to the ladies. Often the ladies' toast is witty with one or two funny stories, but usually it is mostly complimentary about the ladies and thanks them for their support throughout the year. At the end of this speech all of the gentlemen will raise their glasses in a toast to the ladies. This will be followed by a rendition of one of the 'Ladies' Songs'. Different songs are used in some areas so we have given the words to three 'Ladies' Songs' that we are aware of at the end of this chapter. You may like the words to one which isn't normally used in your area and fancy a change. Whichever one you use, the gentlemen normally all join in towards the end and once again stand and raise their glasses to you. It is usually at this point that the ladies' gifts are distributed, but again this may differ from Lodge to Lodge.

At last it is the time of the evening that you, the Lady, have been dreading. It is customary for you to respond on behalf of all of the ladies to the kind words which have been said about them in the ladies' toast. This is probably the biggest worry that you will have about the whole evening, yet it need not be a worry as everyone in the room is on your side and has sympathy with you. It is quite acceptable just simply to stand and say thank you to everyone for joining you on this special evening, but most Ladies feel they want to say a little more.

There is help available if you wish to write a more comprehensive speech. Try visiting *www.presentationhelper.co.uk* or *www.greatspeechwriting.co.uk*.

If you would like help with a rhyming speech it may be worthwhile visiting *www.rhymeonline.co.uk* where, for a small fee, a speech will be written for you all in rhyme!

An example of a rhyming poem is given below and may be used without permission by anyone who thinks it would fit into their speech. If it can help someone, that is a great reward.

Just Once A Month

Just once a month that's all it is
Just twelve nights in the year
With maybe a practice now and then
That's all it is, my dear.

So once a month he trotted off
Black suit, black tie, white shirt
What do they do I asked myself
Won't someone dish the dirt!

It's my Third next month he proudly announced
I might need some help with words
I bet there are several ladies here
Who could easily take their Thirds!

The little blue book goes everywhere
It's read whilst in the bath
Is this because it's the only room
That's properly "Tiled" I asked
I'm joining Chapter Oh and mark
I'm out three times next week
I'll need more shirts than usual dear
Well what a bloomin' cheek!

And so my tale goes on and on
My husband is having a ball
And me I remember what I was told
Just once a month that's all!

Cheryl Skidmore 2008

Lodge Night

Off you go, it's Lodge tonight
A night when I can spend
An evening doing what I like
Alone or with a friend.

These evenings can be pure delight
A 'freedom' if you like
The remote control is in my hand
My dinner's in the mic.

To have just one night in the week
When I can make the choices
A night to catch up with the girls
We can exercise our voices.

I could join the gym
Or maybe jog – I like the sound of that
A fitness night to help me slim
And get rid of excess fat.

Am I lonely? – I ask myself
I don't think that's the case
I enjoy my nights when you're at Lodge
And to see your smiling face

When you come home and tell me all
That you've enjoyed tonight
I know next time you go to Lodge
That I will be all right.

Cheryl Skidmore 2008

As you can see these are very light-hearted and I am sure that many ladies will be able to relate to the sentiments therein!

Another idea is to look at a Masonic alphabet. This may be incorporated into a speech or used just on its own. Here is one that we have written which you may like to use.

A Masonic Alphabet

A is for the Apron, the badge all Masons wear
B is for the Brethren and the Brothers who all care
C is for their Charity, much money they will give
D is for Degrees, the measures by which they live
E is for the East, the place of wisdom and light
F is for the Floor which is chequered black and white
G is for the gloves always worn for every meeting
H is for the Handshake, not the one we use for greeting
I is for Initiate, the newest Brother there
J is for the Journey, one that all the Brothers share
K is for King Solomon, his Temple holds the key
L is for the Lodge, seldom shown to you or me

M is for the Master, the main man of the year
N is for the Numbers – odd or even, do we care?
O is for the Oaths they swore that they would keep
P is for Past Masters who sometimes fall asleep!
Q is for the Questions and the answers that they learn
R is for the Ritual at which each will take their turn
S is for the Sun and the splendour of its rays
T is for the Tools from the mason's working days
U is for Universal brotherhood across the world
V is for the V.S.L. on the pedestal unfurled
W is for the Wardens as they fast approach the chair
X is 'Xceptional' the fellowship they share
Y is for Yesterday from which the future's driven
Z is for the Zealous way the ladies' toast was given.

Cheryl Skidmore 2008

The following poem was written by Mrs Margaret McGhee, the wife of Matt McGhee, Past Master of Powell Lodge No 2257 in the Province of Bristol who very kindly gives us (and you) permission to use it.

The thought of all those evenings alone,
When the Worshipful Master is not at home,
A jacket potato will do for my tea,
I'm not at the Freemasons dining you see.

The hours tick by, I'm nodding my head,
And just about thinking I'll go up to bed,
When suddenly I hear the key in the door,
Who is this chap, I've seen him before,
His face is grinning from ear to ear,
"Had a good night, how are you my dear?"
As I switch off the button to switch off the TV.
He's decided some football he'd just like to see,

Goodnight Worshipful Master, I'm off to bed,
Enjoy the game I sleepily said.

The very next morning drinking tea sat in bed
"Are you out tonight" I gingerly said,
"Well actually John's asked me to dine you see,
So you need not worry about cooking me tea."
The patter goes on week after week,
So an excuse not to cook I constantly seek,
However, the year has almost gone by,
I'll soon have him home, like old times I sigh.

We'll sit side by side like a pigeon pair,
And memories of the past year we'll fondly share,
It just now remains for me to say
Thanks to the many friends we've made on the way,

Ladies enjoy now your special night
Believe me, you've earnt it, I know that I'm right,
Now thank you Brethren for all that you've done,
For making this night such a memorable one.

The following is an anonymous piece that has been handed down over the years.

Thoughts of a Mason's Wife

How many wives of Masons have ever given thought
To the wonderful Biblical lessons that Masonry has taught?
Have you ever asked yourself this question – when you sit alone at night;
While 'hubby' is away at Lodge – Is my reasoning straight and right?
I know the nights are long and lonely – but – the question comes to me
"If my husband wasn't a Mason – what kind of man would he be?"
They call me a Masonic widow – I've been one for many years

I've spoken to my husband after lonely nights – with some berated fears.
But, again I regret my words – and with wisdom try to see
"If my husband wasn't a Mason – what kind of man would he be?"
And so I try to be patient – for long I meditate
And see his point of view as he leaves for Lodge (with these words) "I won't
be late."
Some say that Masonry is good – and this I understand
But, deep in my heart I still maintain "Masonry makes the man."
As we journey the Highway together – to the inner things of life
May their teachings go on for ever.

Sincerely,
A Mason's wife

Another idea, one that can take a great deal of thinking about, is to write
a poem including the names of the Brothers in the Lodge or alternatively one
using the names of the ladies attending the function. This does mean a lot of
hard work, but having heard this kind of speech it is well worth it as the end
result can be quite outstanding.

However you decide to respond to the toast to the ladies, the main thing
is to speak slowly and clearly and use about three focal points in the room
which you can concentrate on. Don't be afraid to pause to gather yourself –
it will seem like an eternity to you, but will be hardly noticeable to your
audience. As we said before, everyone in the room will be willing you on, so
try to enjoy it! If you really don't feel able to make the speech yourself then
you can ask someone to respond on your behalf, maybe a daughter, sister or
a good friend.

At some Ladies' Nights, the Lady's response will be followed by a toast to
the Worshipful Master by one of the Brethren in the Lodge and, of course,
the Master will then respond. Not every Lodge follows this practice and it
may be that at this point the Master will just stand up and say a few words
and maybe present some thank you tokens. Perhaps these would be a bouquet
and/or present to you, his Lady, and sometimes a bouquet to the Festival
Secretary's lady if she has been involved in the organising of the evening or

just to say thank you for allowing her partner to give his time to assist you and also a gift for the Festival Secretary for his help over the past months in arranging everything.

This normally brings the formal part of the evening to an end and the entertainment now commences. During the informal part of the evening the Master and his Lady will normally circulate amongst their guests and speak to people individually, after starting off the dancing, that is.

As the evening draws to a close there are a couple of traditions which may or may not be practised in your particular Lodge. 'Goodnight Ladies' can be quite a lot of fun and can be organised in different ways. It is sometimes done with two circles, one of men and one of ladies. As the music starts the circles move off in opposite directions and when the music stops the lady turns to the gentleman opposite her and gives him a quick kiss goodnight and then they all move off again and repeat the process. The other way it is sometimes done is to have two lines of men forming a column and the ladies move inside the column. When the music stops they turn to the two men whom they are next to and give them a kiss goodnight. When they get to the bottom of the column they move back up the outside ready to go round again. This version usually ends up with lots of laughter as people lose their way or the kissing takes too long!

There are probably lots of other variations on how this can be done. Think of your own and try them out: they might become a new tradition!

At the very end of the evening tradition has us singing 'Auld Lang Syne'. The full version of the words is given below. The Director of Ceremonies will normally (if he is still able to!) get everyone's attention for the Master just to say thank you to everyone for coming and to wish the guests a safe journey home.

A good Ladies' Night is a wonderful experience and one that will be remembered for many years to come. We hope that this chapter has been of some assistance in helping you to think about your Ladies' Night and how you would want people to remember it. Have a lovely evening!

In summary, here is a simple checklist that you may refer to during the evening if you wish:

- Reception
- Presentation of all guests to Master and Lady (photographs to be taken if applicable)
- Guests take seats
- Director of Ceremonies announces Master and escorts him and his Lady to their table.
- Grace
- Commence dinner, taking wine between courses as required
- Chaplain gives thanks
- Remain standing to sing national anthem (first verse)
- First toast of the evening – 'The Queen'
- Toasts, speeches and presentations
- Master and Lady retire from top table and circulate amongst guests
- Dancing – Master and Lady dance the first dance
- At the end of evening
    — Goodnight Ladies' (if used)
    — 'Auld Lang Syne'
    — Final word from the Master who wishes his guests goodnight.

Useful lyrics

'Auld Lang Syne'

Should auld acquaintance be forgot,
And never brought to mind?
Should auld acquaintance be forgot,
And auld lang syne?
Chorus
For auld lang syne, my dear,
For auld lang syne,
We'll tak a cup o' kindness yet,
For auld lang syne!
And surely ye'll be your pint-stowp,
And surely I'll be mine,
And we'll tak a cup o' kindness yet,
For auld lang syne!
We twa hae run about the braes,

And pou'd the gowans fine,
But we've wander'd monie a weary fit,
Sin' auld lang syne.
We twa hae paidl'd in the burn
Frae morning sun till dine,
But seas between us braid hae roar'd
Sin' auld lang syne.
And there's a hand my trusty fiere,
And gie's a hand o' thine,
And we'll tak a right guid-willie waught,
For auld lang syne.
Words adapted from a traditional song
by Robert Burns (1759-96)

'God Save the Queen'
God save our gracious Queen,
Long live our noble Queen
God save the Queen!
Send her victorious,
Happy and glorious,
Long to reign over us:
God save the Queen!

(Second and third verses are rarely used)
O Lord, our God, arise,
Scatter her enemies,
And make them fall:
Confound their politics,
Frustrate their knavish tricks,
On thee our hopes we fix:
God save us all!
Thy choicest gifts in store,
On her be pleased to pour;
Long may she reign:
May she defend our laws,
And ever give us cause
To sing with heart and voice
God save the Queen!

'The Ladies' Song' (Version 1)

Tonight we are met to do Honour,
To those who in sickness and health,
Are Angels who minister to us,
The Ladies our Empire's wealth,
To Mothers, Wives, Sisters and Sweethearts,
True Masons can never do wrong,
We all love the Ladies, God bless them,
And here's to their health in a song.

Chorus – Solo
Here's to their health, here's to their health,
And here's to their health in a song.

Chorus – All gentlemen (standing)
Here's to their health, here's to their health,
And here's to their health in a song.
The Brethren all bid you a welcome,
The night is only for you,
We thank you for all you do for us,
May we always be faithful and true,
The Brethren a Toast to our Ladies,
For our joy in having you here,
We wish you good health and much pleasure,
And happiness all through the year.

Chorus – Solo
Here's to their health, here's to their health,
And here's to their health in a song.
Chorus – All gentlemen (standing)
Here's to their health, here's to their health,
And here's to their health in a song.
To the wife of our Worshipful Master,
Our dutiful homage we pay,
May her joys be as wide as the ocean,

Her sorrows as light as its spray,
The ground that she treads on shall blossom,
Till blessings around her shall throng,
Long life to the Lady we honour,
And here's to her health in a song.

Chorus – Solo
Here's to their health, here's to her health,
And here's to her health in a song.

Chorus – All gentlemen (standing)
Here's to their health, here's to her health,
And here's to her health in a song.

'The Ladies' Song' (Version 2)
When life is sad and dreary,
And heavy with dull care,
And a Brother is full laden,
With troubles hard to bear,
'Til then he looks for comfort,
And solace in the strife,
From the lady whom he worships,
His mother, sweetheart, wife.

Chorus – Solo
Then here's to the Ladies! Our mothers, sweethearts, wives;
They drive our cares and toils away, bring sunshine to our lives;
Then drink to the Ladies! God bless them everyone;
Here's health and happiness to all. The Ladies! The Ladies! The Ladies!
Repeat Chorus – All gentlemen (standing)
How happy is the Brother,
And bless'd with wealth untold
Whose lady is a treasure,
And worth her weight in gold;
Who travels on life's journey

And weathers storm and tide
Who meets life's joys and sorrows
With his loved one by his side.
Chorus – Solo
Repeat Chorus – All gentlemen (standing)

So Brothers, guard them clearly;
Let nothing come amiss;
Console them in their sorrows,
Join them in their bliss
Make happiness their portion,
And drive out grief and tears;
With loving care support them,
Right down throughout the years.
Chorus – Solo
Repeat Chorus – All gentlemen (standing)

'The Ladies' Song' (Version 3)
Ladies from the East and West,
We have done our very best,
To ensure your welcome here,
Bright, Fraternal, and Sincere.

Chorus – Solo
Warm Masonic hearts to meet you,
Hands of Fellowship to greet you,
May our welcome here today,
Cheer each Lady on her way.
Repeat Chorus – All gentlemen (standing)
We all recognise your worth,
Our best friends upon this earth;
May we always be inclined
To be loving, true and kind.

Chorus – Solo
Repeat Chorus – All gentlemen (standing)
When on earth we say "Adieu",
May our love remain with you.
And may we renew that love,
In a Grander Lodge above.

Chorus – Solo
Repeat Chorus – All gentlemen (standing)

Words and music for Ladies' Songs can found by visiting the website of the
Province of Cumberland and Westmorland
www.cumbwestmasons.co.uk/main/songs.shtml
www.ladiesfestivals.net/documents/Ladies Song music.pdf

5

Beyond the Chair

The last ceremony your husband will perform as Master of the Lodge will be the installation of his successor. This is a very important ceremony and you will find him with his head buried in his ritual book preparing for this occasion. Once this is completed your partner will have a sense of relief but also a feeling of anti-climax. So what happens next?

His new title will be Immediate Past Master and his role will be to make sure that the new Master is looked after during his year. He will be prompt for the ceremonies and may be asked to step in if the new Worshipful Master is unable to perform a ceremony for any reason.

Upon leaving the Chair he will become a Past Master. Some Lodges have special jewels which they give to the Immediate Past Master for one year to show their new status within the Lodge. Other Lodges have their own Past Masters' jewels which are presented to all Past Masters and a standard jewel is also available. All Past Masters will have a jewel of some kind to depict their role as a valued member of the Lodge.

Once his year as Immediate Past Master is over, your husband will sit in Lodge as a Past Master and may decide that he would like to take on one of the other roles within the Lodge. There are many that he may consider and a brief description of each is given below.

The Tyler (also known as the Outer Guard of the Lodge)
The Tyler's duty is to guard the Temple door from the outside with a drawn sword and make sure that only those who are qualified manage to enter the Temple. In most Lodges he also prepares candidates for their admission. The Tyler is often a Past Master of the Lodge, while in other jurisdictions where they have no Tyler, he may be a Brother employed from another Lodge. This originates from a historical tradition when Lodges met in taverns and would often employ the landlord as Tyler.

The Secretary

The Secretary is the administrator of the Lodge and his role is the same as the secretarial role in other organisations, with a few additions.

Secretary's emblem

He will maintain all records concerning the members of the Lodge and the ceremonies which they have passed through. He will make returns to his Provincial Grand Lodge and also to the United Grand Lodge of England concerning the number of members and their continued service.

He is responsible for ensuring that all activities carried out within the Lodge meet the requirements of the *Book of Constitutions*, which is the handbook of rules given to all Masons upon their initiation. This includes the proper circulation of the Lodge Summons within the correct timescales. In this age of information technology modern Secretaries will be encouraged wherever possible to use electronic communications, thus saving time, money and the environment.

All activities within the Lodge and communications between the Lodge and Province or United Grand Lodge will be minuted and either read at the next meeting or circulated so that every member has access to them.

The table plan and arrangements for dining will also be looked after by the Secretary, although he may enlist the help of the Assistant Secretary, who may be a Past Master or a more junior member of the Lodge, for some of these duties. In summary, this is a busy role carrying a large responsibility and one which will need a lot of consideration as to the amount of time involved before being undertaken.

The Treasurer

The role of the Treasurer is again similar to that of a treasurer in any society, with the main role being to maintain the Lodge accounts and make full reports to the committee and the Lodge members.

He is responsible for ensuring that the subscriptions are kept at a level that is affordable to members and adequate to make the running of the Lodge viable. Some Lodges include the dining fees in with the Lodge subscriptions and other Lodges have dining fees as a separate amount to be collected at each meeting.

It is imperative that accurate records of membership payments are kept, receipts are issued to members, and that the *Book of Constitutions* is adhered to with regard to non-payment of subscriptions. He will also ensure that all payments due to outside organisations are made as necessary, retaining all receipts and invoices for auditing. He will have to put plans in place to cover any unforeseen expenses as well as the normal and regular expenses that a Lodge will incur.

In conjunction with the Charity Steward he will facilitate donations from the charity account to various charities. He will be responsible for the day-to-day banking arrangements for the Lodge accounts such as paying in to the bank and

Treasurer's emblem

issuing cheques as necessary. He will need to be diligent and organised to keep everything in order and once a year he will be asked to present audited accounts to the Lodge for their approval. In summary, it is a very responsible role which will require time and organisation.

The Director of Ceremonies

The Director of Ceremonies is, as his name suggests, responsible for the structure, accuracy and timing of all ceremonies. From the moment he arrives at Lodge until the end of the Festive Board, the Director of Ceremonies is committed to ensuring the smooth running of the evening. This is one of the most demanding, thankless and, if performed well, one of the most rewarding offices in Freemasonry. The Director of Ceremonies will be the right hand man of the Worshipful Master, offering him support and guidance throughout his year in the Chair and

Director of Ceremonies' emblem

making sure that he is well prepared for his ceremonies. He will also hold Lodge rehearsals to ensure that all Brethren taking part in a ceremony are comfortable with the work they need to do and will give help with ritual where necessary. He will work closely with the Secretary and the Worshipful Master in planning the timetable for the year. In ummary, this is an active role within the Lodge for someone who is a leader, enjoys ritual and working with people.

The Assistant Director of Ceremonies

The Assistant Director of Ceremonies is normally a Director of Ceremonies 'in training' and would normally be the role undertaken first if this is the route which is chosen. He will assist as necessary and a good relationship between himself and the Director of Ceremonies is critical to his development. When it is time for him to take over he, should be well prepared and confident within his role and will already have had some experience of running both the ceremonies within the Lodge room and the formalities afterwards at the Festive Board.

In summary, it is an active role within the Lodge for someone who wishes to learn the duties of the Director of Ceremonies, normally with a view to taking on the higher role within a few years.

The Charity Steward

The Charity Steward is responsible for persuading members of the Lodge to give money for the benefit of other people, without becoming a nuisance. Each member will be encouraged to give only what he is comfortable with. The alms collection made at each Lodge meeting will be his responsibility.

Charity Steward's emblem

The Charity Steward who is enthusiastic and able to communicate well with his fellow Brethren will be the most successful Charity Steward. He will be responsible for ensuring the Lodge achieves any goals set for it by its Province or Group towards any Festival Appeals and will also co-ordinate any charity collections that the Worshipful Master may wish to have.

It is the Charity Steward's job to pass on all relevant information about the various charities to the Lodge to keep Lodge members aware of where any money they are able to give is being used.

Another function of the Charity Steward is to organise or co-ordinate actual fundraising activities for the Lodge members to join in with and for this he may well co-opt a team of willing volunteers. This may be something as simple as asking members to bring raffle prizes or it may be to organise a fundraising event. He will work closely with the Worshipful Master and his Lady to make sure that their wishes are met as well as those of the Lodge. This is a rewarding job and working with other members of the Lodge is vital to achieve success.

The Almoner

This role will be covered in detail in the next chapter as the Almoner is the person who will offer assistance to any Brethren who need to apply to any of the Masonic charities for help. It is important that he is familiar with all the members of the Lodge and he is responsible for looking after any sick or needy Brethren, older members of the Lodge and also any widows of members of the Lodge. The Almoner needs to be discreet and caring and is a highly valued member of the Lodge.

Almoner's emblem

The Chaplain

There are occasions within Masonic Ceremonies when prayers are read. The Chaplain's role is to deliver these prayers with feeling and understanding. The Chaplain does not need to be a man of the cloth but needs to have a sense of what he is saying. His role will be active both in the Lodge room and also at the Festive Board.

There are other offices which may be undertaken by a Past Master. These include Master of Novices, who will encourage, support and teach new Masons at times when they are not permitted to be in the actual ceremony; the Organist who plays for all of the ceremonies; the Assistant Secretary, who could also be a more junior member of the lodge; and a newly formed role of Orator, who delivers lectures within the Lodge when necessary.

Various handbooks are available which cover most of the roles mentioned above should you require further information on any of them.

Provincial Grand Lodge or District Grand Lodge

Every Lodge belongs to a Province or District, which, once a year, holds an annual meeting for all members. At these meetings various honours are awarded for service to individual Lodges or work within the Province. All of the roles within the Lodge also have Provincial equivalents and these roles can be either acting or past rank.

Provincial apron

The Provincial Grand Master will chair these meetings and assisted by the team will make the presentations in front of representatives from the whole area. This is the highlight of the Provincial Masonic year with Masonic dignitaries from other areas often attending and a large number of Brethren supporting the recipients.

Acting Ranks

The Brethren receiving acting ranks have been chosen for the work that they have done or work that they will do in the future for the good of Freemasonry. They are expected to visit Lodges throughout the Province and attend formal events organised by the Province. Actual duties will vary from area to area, but depending on the size of the Province and the number of acting ranks given this can be a big commitment. It is a great honour to be part of the Provincial team and although ranks are usually only acting for one year, Wardens, Director of Ceremonies and Assistant Director of Ceremonies often work on the circuit for a number of years visiting Lodges and assisting in the installations.

The more administrative roles such as Secretary and Treasurer are different and are normally appointed for longer periods to achieve some continuity in the running of a Province. The holders of these posts are recognised in a different way which will be explained later.

Past Ranks

There are many people who deserve acknowledgement for the work they do in Freemasonry and as there are only a limited number of acting ranks available, past ranks are given to recognise this work. As the holder of a past rank your partner may be asked to represent the Province at a chosen Lodge throughout the year and he will be welcomed by this Lodge as a guest of honour.

Over a period of years Brethren may receive promotions to higher ranks in recognition of the work they do for their Lodge, the Province and Freemasonry in general.

All Provincial ranks are normally prompted in the first instance by a committee of Senior Past Masters from a Lodge. If your better half is lucky enough to be honoured it is a great achievement and one of which he will be very proud.

Grand Rank

Grand Rank is in every respect similar to Provincial rank inasmuch as there are both acting and past ranks. However, acting ranks are very rare and so in most cases past ranks are awarded.

Grand Rank is only awarded to a relatively small number of Masons. Usually this is a result of senior Provincial officers such as Provincial Secretaries, Provincial Treasurers and the acting Wardens committing their efforts to the Province over a period of time. There are other occasions when Grand Rank may be given and these will differ from country to country.

It is a very great honour to receive Grand Rank and in the United Kingdom an annual meeting is held in London when recipients from across the country will attend to receive their honours from the Grand Master or the Pro. Grand Master.

And so there it is: a Masonic career in a nutshell.

We hope that in writing this book we may have helped to answer some of the questions you had in relation to Freemasonry. It seems that in some cases the men are still reluctant to discuss their Freemasonry with their partner and as a result some ladies can have feelings of resentment towards something they know very little about. Maybe now you know that he really isn't getting into any mischief, but is merely working towards making himself a better man. In doing so, your husband will help raise money for charity; allow him his 'secrets', share in his achievements and your nights at the Lodge!

6

Masonic Charities, Help and Support

It is said that Masons look after their own. Is this a bad thing?

We would like to start this chapter by telling you a short story that epitomises what Freemasonry is about.

A young man passed a pawnbroker's shop and noticed the pawnbroker standing in front wearing a large and beautiful Masonic emblem. The young man walked on, obviously deep in thought, and after some time he turned and went back to the pawnbroker and said, "I note that you are wearing a Masonic emblem. I too am a Freemason, and I am in urgent need of 50 dollars. You don't know me, but I wonder whether the fact that we are Freemasons is sufficient for you to lend me the money. I would repay you within ten days."

The pawnbroker mentally appraised the young man, who was clean cut, neat and well dressed, and after a moment's thought agreed to make the loan on the strength of the Masonic connection.

Within a few days the young man returned and repaid the loan, and that was the end of the transaction.

For some time after, the young man thought of the pawnbroker and how readily he had lent him the 50 dollars, and he said to himself, "If that is the spirit of Freemasonry, I'll join."

He made application, and in due course attended to receive his Entered Apprentice degree. After the degree, when he was duly seated, he looked across the room, and there was the pawnbroker! After the meeting, he tried to avoid the pawnbroker and leave as soon as possible; but the pawnbroker recognised him, and approached him with an outstretched hand and a smile saying, "So you weren't a Freemason when I lent you the 50 dollars."

"No, I wasn't," stammered the young man. "But I wish you would let me explain. I had always heard that Freemasons were charitable, and would help a Brother in need. I had no need of the 50 dollars, but when I saw the Masonic emblem you were wearing, I thought it would be a good opportunity to learn whether what I had heard about the Freemasons was true. You lent me the money on the strength of my being a Freemason, and I was so impressed that I decided to join the order and here I am. I trust that you will forgive me for deceiving you."

The pawnbroker smiled and said, "Don't let that worry you. I wasn't a Freemason when I lent you the money. I shouldn't have been wearing the emblem, but another man had just borrowed some money on it, and it looked so pretty that I put it in my lapel for a few minutes. When you asked for the 50 dollars, I recollected what I had heard about Freemasons: that they were honest, trustworthy, and kept their promises faithfully. I thought that it would be worth 50 dollars to find out if what I had heard was true. So I lent you the money and when you came so promptly to repay it, I was so impressed that I decided to join the Order. I was the candidate before you." *Author unknown*

Charity is one of the fundamental principles of Freemasonry. All money raised is donated by Masons and their friends and family: you do not see a Mason standing on a street corner rattling a collection tin. Many of the charities supported are the Masons' own charities which we will cover in a moment, but Masons also give millions of pounds away each year to non-Masonic charities.

Non-Masonic charities

Non-Masonic charities in England and Wales benefit from the generosity of grants made by the Freemasons' Grand Charity.

Since 1984, over £7 million has been donated towards the operating costs of hospice services across England and Wales, and in March 2008, it was announced that a further £600,000 was to be awarded to adult and children's hospice services.

A further £180,000 is to be awarded to air ambulance charities during this year alone and further grants will be awarded to other charities throughout the year.

During 2007, major grants totalled over £3 million and helped charities supporting medical research, youth opportunities and vulnerable people. Individual grants are normally for sums between £10,000 and £25,000 although grants of up to £50,000 may be considered. Minor grants for charities supporting the same areas, but with smaller annual incomes are awarded up to £5000. As an example, please find details below of grants approved in October 2007 to see the wide diversity of charities which received assistance. Details can be obtained from Grand Charity: *www.grandcharity.org*.

Medical research

Leukaemia Research Fund (£56,000)
To fund research at the University of Kent into acute myeloid leukaemia (AML) and to develop a new technique of radioimmunotherapy for treating patients. AML is an aggressive cancer affecting nearly 2,000 people in the UK each year. The project will prepare for a clinical trial enabling cancer cells to be targeted more effectively.

The Healing Foundation (£30,200)
To fund research into Dupuytren's disease at Imperial College, London. Dupuytren's disease is a condition affecting older people whereby the fingers curl up to the palm, causing loss of function.

Vulnerable people

The Place2Be (£75,000 over three years)
A grant to fund a new service at six primary schools in Burnley and the publication of an information leaflet. The Place2Be helps disadvantaged young children to cope with the problems caused by abuse, parental drug and alcohol problems, domestic violence and bullying by providing a therapist and counselling service within primary schools in deprived areas.

British Institute for Brain Injured Children (£30,000)
To fund an upgrade of the IT equipment for staff. BIBIC treats children with neurological disorders at special clinics. It provides a multi-disciplinary team of therapists and medical staff to assess and design therapeutic treatment programmes for parents to deliver at home to help improve the quality of life for disabled children and their families.

Listening Books (£30,000 over two years)
To fund the Digital Book project converting the cassette audiobook library for disabled people into digital format for use on MP3, CD players and via Internet streaming. Listening Books provides over 2,000 titles free of charge to more than 4,000 disabled children and adults.

Aidis Trust (£20,000 over two years)
To fund specialist disability-related information and communication technology training for staff and volunteers in local grass-roots disability organisations and hospices. The project will improve the use of computer and technology equipment by and for disabled people by providing advice and support on special adaptations.

The Challenging Behaviour Foundation (£12,000)
To part-fund a family information service. The foundation provides evidence of how best to manage the challenging and sometimes violent or destructive behaviour of people with severe learning disabilities and supports families who are dealing with children or young people who exhibit such disruptive behaviour.

Youth opportunities

The Marine Society and Sea Cadets (£47,000)
A grant to contribute towards a new training ship to be berthed in London. Each year 640 young people, many of them from deprived areas, will benefit from a six-day training voyage as Sea Cadets on the new vessel.

Voice for the Child in Care (£40,000)
To fund a pilot project aimed at improving access to the independent advocacy services for children in foster care and privately run children's homes. Many of the 60,000 children in care are currently hard to reach and are not aware of, or are unable to access, the independent services that are available to support them.

Phoenix Futures (£30,000)
To part-fund a skills and employability programme for young people in residential drug and alcohol rehabilitation centres. The charity helps about 13,000 people each year and runs six adult residential services for over 700 people, providing a therapeutic community recovery programme and support in moving into education, training or employment.

Childhood First (£25,000)
To fund a support package for young people leaving a Childhood First residential care home, providing training for independent living and ongoing support for 12 months after the young people leave. The charity runs five residential facilities for children who cannot be placed through the normal care system due to severe emotional or behavioural disturbance.

Happy Days Children's Charity (£24,500)
To fund day trips for children with special needs from disadvantaged backgrounds. The charity provides holidays or outings for over 12,000 children with special needs each year.

Religious buildings

Guildford Cathedral (£5,000)
A grant to Guildford Cathedral for the West Window Appeal.

St Woolos Cathedral (£5,000)
A grant to St Woolos Cathedral, Newport, for the Rescue Appeal.
From time to time, the Freemasons' Grand Charity supports overseas charities through grants to the appropriate District Grand Lodge. In 2007, the District Grand Lodge of Ghana received a grant of £10,000 towards the purchase of an electromyogram machine for the Korle-Bu Teaching Hospital in Accra. The machine will be used for the diagnosis and management of patients with nerve and muscle disorders. It is the only one of its kind available to public health institutions in Ghana and will help to cut long waiting periods for patients and reduce the need to travel abroad for treatment for people from Korle-Bu and across the entire West African Sub-region.

The machine was officially handed over to Korle-Bu Teaching Hospital by The Grand Master, HRH the Duke of Kent, and the District Grand Master, Kow Abaka Quansah, during an official visit by The Grand Master to mark the celebration of 50 years of Ghanaian independence.

The Grand Charity also makes emergency grants to areas where disaster has struck. During recent years one of the largest donations was that to the Red Cross of £100,000 for the Tsunami Appeal. Other worldwide donations made include over £27,000 to the Hurricane Katrina fund, £104,503 to the South Asia Earthquake fund, £50,000 to relief in the conflict in Darfur, £65,000 to the UK Floods Appeal and in 2008, £10,000 to the Kenyan crisis. Grants in excess of £1.7 million have been made since 1981 (all information and figures correct as of 4 February 2008 and taken from United Grand Charity website: *www.grandcharity.org*).

A glance at the spring 2008 edition of *Freemasonry Today*, a quarterly magazine available to all Freemasons and the official journal of the United Grand Lodge of England, will give you an idea of some of the fundraising activities in recent months. It is well worthwhile 'borrowing' your partner's magazine to have a look through. This quarter covers the donation of £40,000 to the families of four firefighters who lost their lives in the call of duty. This is a donation by a Province and Provinces across the country who have their own charities which they support in addition to the donations made by the Grand Charity. You will also read about individual Lodges supporting their local communities. In this particular edition of *Freemasonry Today*, there is a feature about a Lodge in Staffordshire, England, which has purchased 75 high-visibility safety jackets for its local school so that pupils may go on school outings. This shows that Masons are also active in their local communities.

Working with local charities is usually the choice of the Worshipful Master who may adopt a charity for his year in the Chair. In this way a wide range of charities may benefit from the generosity of the Masons. Whether it be the local church, school, dogs' home or bereavement group, they will all greatly appreciate the support that is given to them. This is also a brilliant opportunity for the ladies to get involved themselves and join in the local fundraising activities. Quite often a social event will be the way money is raised so you get double benefits! A group of Lodges locally recently hosted a pantomime for children from bereaved families. Working closely with the organisers of the group, the children were invited to the local Lodge rooms for an afternoon's entertainment by a travelling pantomime company. To be able to witness their smiling faces was a just reward for the work and money that had gone into organising the event.

When Mark Master Masons celebrated the 150th anniversary of their Grand Lodge, they presented a cheque for £3 million to the National Osteoporosis Society to fund a major project to provide mobile diagnostic and treatment facilities to cover areas where reasonable access to hospitals is lacking. Is this just helping their own?

In Ireland, £400,000 was raised to set up the Freemasons of Ireland Medical Research Fund from which grants of over £200,000 have already been awarded. Sufferers from Alzheimer's disease are now benefiting from an appeal which raised £500,000 and local hospitals benefit from donations from individual Lodges.

Freemasons also support:

Lifelites

Through the power of technology and high tech entertainments, Lifelites is a charity striving to give children in hospices the chance to spend quality time with their families, the means to keep in contact with their school and friends, and simply to enjoy themselves away from the constant reality of their illness. *www.lifelites.org*

TLC Appeal –Teddies for Loving Care (Registered Charity 1087765)

TLC provides teddies and soft toys to accident and emergency units for the staff to give, at their discretion, to children who are in distress, when the staff feel that a teddy to cuddle will help alleviate that anguish and assist them in their urgent work. The children can then take the teddies home with them.

The appeal originated after an allergic reaction suddenly caused the swelling and blocking of the windpipe of the wife of an Essex Freemason. Her life was saved by the rapid action of the medical staff at an A&E unit, who were able to resuscitate and stabilise her. They are both eternally grateful for the swift and caring attention that she received, but found the experience the most frightening of their lives and speculated on the distress that children must face when visiting

A&E units.

The Mason asked members of his Lodge and other local Freemasons to help to do something useful as a thank you to the A&E unit and its staff. From that point the idea of Teddies for Loving Care was born. From a recent TCL press release:

> *Just over 7 years ago, Essex Masons launched a scheme at Essex A&E units called 'TLC' – Teddies for Loving Care. The idea was simple. When a child is in severe distress at an A&E unit, they can be difficult to treat and the whole experience can be frightening and very stressful. Produce a TLC Teddy for them to look at, cuddle, or whatever is appropriate, and the whole situation calms down, and often turns to smiles when they are told they can keep the Teddy! The idea was so successful that it was not long before it spread up and down the country and overseas. Over 37 counties now also operate the scheme and it also operates in Gibraltar, Cyprus, and even the USA!'*

To date over 500,000 teddies have been given to distressed children at A&E units all over the world!

The TLC Appeal is a registered charity No 1087765 and facilitates the appeals' activities in Essex and elsewhere. It is run on an entirely voluntary basis and ninety-nine per cent funded by Freemasons.

The Patron of TLC is Peter Lowndes, Deputy Grand Master of the United Grand Lodge of England, with John Webb, Provincial Grand Master of Essex, as Vice Patron and Ian Simpson, Chairman.

Masons tend not to publicise their generosity like other fundraising groups and people are often unaware of the wonderful work that they do. So let it not be said that Masons only look after their own! *ww.tlcappeal.org*

Masonic charities

There are four main charities in place to support Masons and their families. These are known as the Central Masonic Charities and they have just moved into purpose-designed accommodation within Freemasons' Hall. They now employ over 100 staff, and all of the charities are able to work much closer together to provide the best possible support available for Freemasons and their families.

A Legacy Appeal was announced in 2006 to promote legacy-giving for the benefit of these four charities. Their valuable work covers the areas of education, healing and financial support in cases of hardship. We are including details of these charities as we have found that many Masons, let alone their wives or partners, are unaware of the help and support available. In times of trouble it is usually your family that rallies round to support you and in this sense the help available is from your Masonic family should it be needed.

The Royal Masonic Benevolent Institution (RMBI)

Statement of purpose
The Royal Masonic Benevolent Institution seeks to offer high quality care, support and assistance to older Freemasons and their dependants. We are committed to ensuring the individuals' right to dignity, respect, choice and control over their lives is upheld and maintained.

Aims
We currently operate 17 residential homes across England and Wales offering a range of high quality care options, including residential and nursing care, dementia support and respite care. We also provide advice for those who are in difficulty but who wish to remain in their own homes. The homes cover a variety of needs:

- Nursing care provides care for people with specific medical conditions, who require treatment under the direction of a Registered Nurse.

- Dementia care is a specialised area of care which caters for people with some form of mental frailty such as Alzheimer's disease or other forms of dementia.

- Sheltered accommodation offering a limited amount of such accommodation for older people who are able to manage in their own home but prefer to live in a sheltered community, where they can remain independent but with support nearby in an emergency.

- Respite care is short-term care, which can give people caring for someone full-time a well-earned break. It is also a good way of sampling life in a care home when considering a permanent move into care. In conjunction with the new Masonic Samaritan Fund, a pilot scheme has been launched offering respite care normally for one or two weeks at a time to give the carer a much needed break, safe in the knowledge that their loved one is in good hands. Respite will be available as an ongoing support as and when it is needed. As with all applications for assistance each case is considered individually.

One of the principal objectives of the RMBI is to help needy Freemasons and their dependants by payment of an annuity. In April 2002, the responsibility for administering the current RMBI annuities was taken over by the Grand Charity, with the payment of grants to existing recipients being met from investment funds transferred from the RMBI to the Grand Charity.

This step means that the Grand Charity has assumed responsibility for all future grants to Freemasons and their dependants who require financial assistance to help them through difficult times.

Additional funds have been raised for the RMBI by the Royal Masonic Variety Show in which artists such as Jim Davidson, Bradley Walsh and Roger de Courcey, to name but a few, give their time for free to raise money for the RMBI, along with the Entertainment Artists Benevolent Fund and the Abandoned and Destitute Children's Appeal Fund. More information can be found by visiting the website: *www.rmbi.org.uk*

The Royal Masonic Trust for Girls and Boys (RMTGB)

On 25 March 1808, The Duchess of Cumberland and Chevalier Bartholomew Ruspini, a prominent Freemason, opened a school for children which laid the foundations for what was to eventually become the Royal Masonic Trust for Girls and Boys on 1 May 2003. Over the last 200 years, the needs of Freemasons and their families have been met by the fund with the aim of relieving poverty wherever possible and providing an education for life for its beneficiaries.

The RMTGB supports the children of Freemasons who have died, have a disability, are suffering financially or have deserted their families for whatever reason, and undertakes to provide them with the level of education their father would have wanted. There are various grants, scholarships and bursaries available to help young people continue their education. A family maintenance allowance is paid each term and funds are also provided to assist with school trips, school uniforms, and in some cases short holidays. In 2005, over 2000 girls and boys were supported either in school, college or university and this number continues to grow.

The trust will also look after other children with no Masonic connections if money permits and will support applications from schools which represent individual children whom they feel would benefit from the financial support of the trust, in particular by continuing to offer bursaries at cathedrals and choral foundations. Each case is considered on its own merits.

The RMTGB also supports children's hospices across the country by ensuring that all hospices have access to information technology, with local Masons giving ongoing support with technical help in many instances. This of course helps to develop a great community spirit and gives great personal satisfaction to the individuals involved. For more information visit the website: *www.rmtgb.org*

**The Masonic Samaritan Fund
(Registered Charity 1001298)**
The MSF is a young charity. It was established in 1990 to take on the role of the Samaritan Fund at the Royal Masonic Hospital. Since the hospital was closed and sold in 1996, it has been the only central Masonic charity that funds the provision of medical care and support. The Masonic Samaritan Fund helps those who:

Medical Care and Support

• Have an identified medical need
• Are waiting for treatment on the NHS
• Are unable to afford private treatment.

Support is available to Freemasons (anyone who at any time has been initiated into or joined a Lodge under the English Constitution) and their wives, partners, widows and dependants.

In each of the last few years, the support provided by the fund has been split almost equally between Freemasons and their wives, widows, partners and dependants. There are no age limits – to date they have funded applicants from 6 months to 104 years! There is no qualifying period of membership and no requirement for the Freemason to still be active in the Craft.

Potential applicants are encouraged to make early contact with the fund for further details and the latest information. The following definitions may help to answer some questions:

Identified medical need:
Applicants need to have seen a consultant who has made a diagnosis and identified a course of treatment, medical aid or surgery.

Waiting for treatment:
A wait of three months or more (two months or more for cardiac surgery) is considered by the fund to be a long wait.

Partners:
Someone who is living with a Freemason 'as if married' or was at the time of his death. This applies equally to same-sex partnerships.

Dependants:
Someone who is physically or financially dependent on a Freemason or his estate. This is straightforward in the case of school-age children living at home, but can extend beyond this immediate family. The mother of a Freemason, for example, who lives with her son, may be eligible to apply.

Financial need:
Applicants do not need to be destitute to qualify for assistance. In establishing the financial need, account will be taken of both income and capital (of both husband and wife if appropriate), but will not include the value of your main residence. Account will be taken of the value of any additional properties owned. Allowances are made for reasonable living expenses and for modest savings. The likely cost of the proposed treatment is also deducted from any capital. Some applicants may be asked to make a contribution towards the overall cost of treatment.

With minor exceptions, if licensed by the NHS, the MSF will consider applications for all kinds of medical treatment which include surgical, medical, ophthalmic, gynaecological, IVF, orthopaedic, cardiac, diagnostic (includes scan, angiograms, etc), urological, specialised dental and hearing related treatment. Applications for grants for medication relating to the treatment of cancer and degenerative diseases are also considered.

Once an application is accepted, the interests of the patient are paramount and the required treatment will be obtained at whichever hospital is the most appropriate and, if possible, near to where the patient lives.

The application process is straightforward and confidential. A Visiting Brother will be appointed to help complete the application forms and to confirm the financial details of the applicant. This will usually involve the Almoner of the member's Lodge. However, if the applicant prefers not to disclose personal information to a member of their own Lodge a Visiting Brother can be appointed from another Lodge or Province.

Potential applicants are welcome to make direct contact with the fund in order to determine eligibility. Only in exceptional circumstances will the fund support applications made after treatment has been booked. Early contact, by phone, letter or e-mail, is therefore essential. Initial enquiries are welcome from Almoners or potential applicants.

The fund has a variety of publicity material available and is very happy to provide a speaker to talk about the work of the fund in the hope that all eligible applicants are aware of what may be available.

If an applicant has a long wait for a consultation appointment on the NHS they may opt for a private consultation at their own expense. Only in exceptional circumstances, if either the Lodge or Province the applicant is associated with cannot cover the cost of the private consultation, will the MSF consider reimbursement when an application for a grant is received. Following a private consultation it remains in the applicant's best interests to also remain on the NHS waiting list. If an application to the MSF is unsuccessful, the applicant will still hopefully have made progress up the NHS waiting list.

The applicant should hear within four weeks of presenting a fully completed application. Once approval has been given and any contribution required has been paid, the fund authorises treatment and accepts responsibility for the cost including all hospital charges.

Respite Care

Caring for a partner, child, relative, friend or neighbour who could not manage on their own, possibly due to age, physical or mental illness, addiction or disability, is often a full-time job. As with any other job, the carer is likely to benefit from some time away from their caring responsibilities in order to return refreshed to 'work'.

Many people with caring responsibilities do not consider themselves to be a carer. They are looking after their spouse, parent or child and just getting on with the role as anyone else would in the same situation. Yet of the six million carers in this country, over 59% suffer from deteriorating health because the type and intensity of care needed can compromise their own health and well-being. The MSF will support applications to fund the provision of respite care so that the carer can take a well-earned rest, confident that their loved one is being looked after in a safe and caring environment. This support has been available for over two years and can be provided either in an RMBI care home or at a private residential care home near to where the applicant lives. Repeat applications are welcomed and expected as the care need continues.

Applications remain subject to a confidential assessment of financial need and a response can be provided quickly. If you are caring for a loved one and feel that you would benefit from a break, please contact the Fund for further details.

Respite care is available to those who have a long-term caring commitment and should not be confused with convalescent care. The latter is usually associated with a period of care to assist with recuperation after surgery or a stay in hospital. The MSF does not currently consider applications for convalescent care. Any enquiries for support should be directed first to the medical professional who has advised that convalescence is required. For further information telephone the Fund on 020 7404 1550 or visit *www.msfund.org.uk.*

The Grand Charity

The Grand Charity is the main grant-giving charity of all Freemasons in the English Constitution. Every year, the Freemasons' Grand Charity awards grants to thousands of needy individuals. Support for Masons and their dependants is one of the primary activities of the charity and no case of genuine need is ever rejected.

- Grants given towards the cost of living expenses and unexpected needs
- There is no limit to the number of grants an individual may receive over their lifetime
- Annual grants usually range from £350 to £4,500.

Any Freemason experiencing genuine hardship may apply – even if he no longer belongs to a Lodge — as can his immediate dependants or widow. Grants are renewed annually and will continue until financial need ends. As with all of the funds, applications for assistance are carefully considered. Applications will be rejected if savings of £10,000 (£15,000 for a couple) are held, but house values are ignored. A decision is usually reached within 4-6 weeks of the application being received.

Each year the Grand Charity assists nearly 2000 Masonic families with grants which range from £300 to £4000 at a total cost of £2.6 million. Each month consideration is given to around 183 applications.

The Grand Charity also manages a scheme for the free loan of mobility equipment such as stair lifts, mobility scooters and wheelchairs. Equipment is carefully chosen to meet the needs of the user and is supplied in partnership with an outside agency, the Keep Able Group. Details of this scheme can be found on the website: *www.grandcharity.org.*

The Freemasons' Grand Charity also has the unique responsibility of providing financial support to the other central Masonic Charities when justifiable needs are identified.

All four Masonic charities are supported by Masons across England and Wales and different Provinces will run Festival Appeals with one of the charities as beneficiary. These Festivals run for a specific period of time and have a target sum to be raised. A Festival launched today might be entitled Festival 2013, which means that a period of five years will be given to raise the targeted sum.

For the duration of the Festival this will become the priority charity and both the Province and individual Lodges will hold fundraising events. Sponsored walks, bike rides and runs will be organised along with quiz nights, musical nights and any other kind of night that you can think of which will raise funds.

Merchandise such as cufflinks, braces, ties or trolley coins will be available which will be sold on behalf of the appeal and everyone will be encouraged to support it in some way.

The Festival may culminate with or sometimes be launched by a Festival Ball which will normally be hosted by the Provincial Grand Master and all proceeds will be for the fund – an occasion to look forward to!

We hope that now you are more informed about the charity work which your husband or partner is involved in you will feel able to take a more active role in supporting this work, or at least be able to appreciate the work which our men do.

We have detailed various help that is available to you through your wider Masonic family, but how would you go about accessing any of this help? Who would you turn to?

The Almoner

Any application for assistance should be made through the Lodge Almoner who will have access to contacts and appropriate forms for completion. It may be necessary to divulge certain financial details to him and for this reason he must be totally discreet in all of his dealings. But who is the Almoner?

Within each Lodge an Almoner is appointed. He is usually a Mason with years of knowledge and experience and who has been elected by the Lodge as a person who is caring, approachable, diligent and discreet and therefore suitable to take on this important role. A younger man may take on the role, but will not have the experience of the older gentleman as the Almoner needs to know all of the members of the Lodge and be aware of their personal circumstances with regards to their health and well-being. This job requires a person with a great deal of patience and diplomacy, as some Masons will find it really difficult to ask for help and at a time when they are feeling vulnerable or under pressure will need to be handled very carefully. The Almoner's role is to look after the welfare of the members of the Lodge and their families, offering assistance during illnesses or difficult times.

The Almoner will be aware of elderly Brethren who are no longer able to drive themselves to Lodge and will arrange lifts for them. Some of them may no longer be able to attend Lodge and a visit from the Almoner to keep them updated on Lodge activities will help to keep them involved. The Almoner can also encourage other members of the Lodge to visit them to make them feel valued as members of the Lodge. In the same way widows of members of the Lodge will be visited and kept an eye on by the caring Almoner.

In time of sickness the Almoner will keep other Brethren of the Lodge informed as to the progress of their sick Brother or member of his family. He will be aware of any needs the Brother's family may have, even if it is only to offer a lift to a wife who is unable to drive to visit her sick husband or needs help with the shopping. Sometimes the support needed can be much more involved and the Almoner will assist in the best way to suit the family. It may be that the family has friends also associated with the Lodge with whom they would prefer to discuss matters and in

these circumstances the Almoner would just oversee everything to make sure help was given if needed.

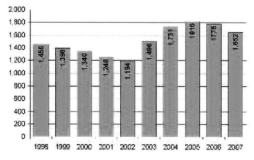

Grand Charity graph

It would also be the Almoner who would give advice and support in the event of bereavement. Such a sensitive matter needs to be handled very carefully and a discreet but supportive friend can be found in most Almoners. The Almoner continues to care for any widows of members of the Lodge, visiting them and making sure that they are well cared for after their partner's death. He will also make sure that they are invited to social functions and arrange lifts for them if they wish to attend and do not have their own transport.

Whatever the circumstances, if you feel that you need support for you and your family, contact the Almoner who will give all the help he can. In complicated cases he may need to contact the Provincial Almoner for guidance. So yes, Masons do look after their own – and it is not a bad thing!

My Last Degree

An old man lay sick in the Masonic Home.
His face was as wan as the white sea foam.
His eyes were dim, his hair was gray,
His back was bent with the trials of the way.
He faltering spoke, but I heard him say,
"I'm ready for my last degree."

"I've come to the end of the level of time
That leads us all to that Grand Lodge sublime
From whose bourn none ever return.
More light in Masonry there I shall learn
By an Altar where light shall evermore shine,
I'm ready for my last degree.

"With the Apprentice's gauge, I've divided my time
Into three equal parts since life's early prime.
And this I have found amidst life's great turmoil,
My wages are due me, in Corn, Wine and Oil.
I'm ready for my last degree.

"Each day from life's quarries, I've hewn a stone,
With the gavel I've shaped them, each one alone,
And shipped them along beyond that bright stand,
To build me a house in that great better land.
A spiritual house not made with hands.
I'm ready for my last degree.

"I've squared each stone by the virtue square,
And plumbed them all true, as I shipped them there.
With the compass I've measured the Master's designs
And kept within due bounds, with his points and his lines.
My blueprints are folded, I've answered his signs.
I'm ready for my last degree.

"The mortar I've made, from friendship and love,
To be spread with the Master's trowel up above.
My apron is worn, but its surface is white.
My working tools now will be cold and quiet.
My Trestle Board's bare, and I'm going tonight.
I'm ready for my last degree."

A few moments later, the old man was dead.
And I fancy that I could see his soul as it fled,
Upward and onward, to the great door,
Where he gave an alarm, and a voice did implore.
The old man gave his answer with these words once more,
"I'm ready for my last degree."

That night in a Lodge, free from all strife and storm,
He took that degree, his last in due form.
So may I live like he did, to build, day by day,
A spiritual house in that land far away.
So I, when I meet my Grand Master, can say,
"I'm ready for my last degree."

Further Information and Contacts

Listed below are the details of various organisations, publications and suppliers of masonic books and regalia, everything a new or well-established Mason may need.

Organisations

United Grand Lodge of England (UGLE)
Freemasons' Hall
60 Great Queen Street
London
WC2B 5AZ
Tel: +44 (0)20 7831 9811
www.ugle.org.uk

Supreme Grand Chapter of Royal Arch Masons of England
Freemasons' Hall
60 Great Queen Street
London
WC2B 5AZ
www.grandchapter.org.uk

Masonic Research
Canonbury Masonic Research Centre
Canonbury Tower
Canonbury Place
Islington
London
N1 2NQ
www.canonbury.ac.uk

Sheffield University Centre for Masonic Research
Centre for Research into Freemasonry
University of Sheffield
34 Gell Street
Sheffield
S3 7QY
Tel: 0114 222 9890
www.freemasonry.dept.shef.ac.uk

The Cornerstone Society
The Cornerstone Society offers free membership to Master Masons and above to join its forum to discuss the meaning and relevance of Freemasonry.
www.cornerstonesociety.com

Quatuor Coronati Lodge of Research
Quatuor Coronati Correspondence Circle (QCCC) is the premier Masonic Research Lodge in the world.
www.quatuorcoronati.com

Masonic Charities

The Grand Charity
60 Great Queen Street
London
WC2B 5AZ
Tel: 020 7395 9261
E-mail: info@the-grand-charity.org
www.grandcharity.org

The Royal Masonic Trust for Girls and Boys
60 Great Queen Street
London
WC2B 5AZ
Tel: 020 7405 2644
E-mail: info@rmtgb.org
www.rmtgb.org

The Royal Masonic Benevolent Institution
60 Great Queen Street
London
WC2B 5AZ
Tel: 020 7596 2400
E-mail: enquiries@rmbi.org.uk
www.rmbi.org.uk

Masonic Samaritan Fund
60 Great Queen Street
London
WC2B 5AZ
E-mail: mail@msfund.org.uk
www.msfund.org.uk

TLC Appeal - Teddies for Loving Care
TLC Appeal
54 Medway Crescent
Leigh on Sea
Essex
SS9 2UY
E-mail: info@tlcappeal.org

The Library and Museum of Freemasonry
The Library and Museum of Freemasonry houses one of the finest collections of Masonic material in the world. It is open to the public, Monday to Friday, free of charge. It is a Registered Charity No 1058497.

The museum contains an extensive collection of objects with Masonic decoration including pottery and porcelain, glassware, silver, furniture and clocks, jewels and regalia. Items belonging to famous and royal Freemasons including Winston Churchill and Edward VII are on display together with examples from the museum's extensive collection of prints and engravings, photographs and ephemera.

The library and archives are open for reference use. They contain a comprehensive collection of printed books and manuscripts on Freemasonry in England as well as material on Freemasonry elsewhere in the world and on subjects associated with Freemasonry or with mystical and esoteric traditions. For details of exhibitions, events, tours and genealogical enquiries please see the official website of the Library and Museum.

Freemasons' Hall
60 Great Queen Street
London
WC2B 5AZ
www.freemasonry.london.museum

Publications

Book of Constitutions

All new Masons should be given a copy of the *Book of Constitutions*. However, the most recent edition is available for download in PDF format as a read-only document. The book has been split into six sections for ease of downloading and is available from *www.ugle.org.uk/pdf/index.htm*

Ritual books

Ritual books are available from your Lodge or from all good Masonic booksellers (see below).

Freemasonry Today *www.freemasonrytoday.com*

Freemasonry Today is the official magazine of the United Grand Lodge of England. Previously published independently, *Freemasonry Today* was in circulation from 1997 to 2007 with a run of 42 editions. The United Grand Lodge of England had its own house magazine called *MQ* which was launched in April 2002 with 23 issues published. It was decided to merge both magazines under one banner, keeping the name of *Freemasonry Today*. Therefore, subscriptions to *Freemasonry Today* no longer apply as this magazine will be sent free to subscribing members in England and Wales. Because of the substantial postal costs involved, distribution of the magazine to members of Lodges overseas had to be suspended. The new website will give them access to the magazine, and will also make it available to the general public who surf the web. The first issue of the new *Freemasonry Today* magazine was launched in January 2008. The MQ website is still live so that you can look up previous copies of the magazine. *www.mqmagazine.co.uk*

The Square

An independent magazine for Freemasons published by Lewis Masonic, an imprint of Ian Allan Publishing. *www.ianallanmagazines.com/thesquare*

Suppliers of books, Masonic regalia and gifts

Lewis Masonic is a long-established firm, founded in 1886, specialising in the publication of Masonic texts. Nowadays, ritual books are still kept a priority at Lewis Masonic, but the company's focus has expanded to cover all areas of Masonic publishing.
Lewis Masonic
4 Watling Drive
Hinckley
LE10 3EY
www.lewismasonic.com

The Freemason
Suppliers of Masonic regalia, books, gifts and furnishings for the Lodge. One of the largest and most popular Masonic forums online.

Central Building
Worcester Road,
Stourport on Severn
Worcestershire
DY13 9AS
Tel: 0870 922 0352
E-mail: sales@thefreemason.com
www.thefreemason.com

Letchworth's –The Shop at Freemasons' Hall
The shop sells gifts, stationery, postcards and souvenirs of Freemasons' Hall, many with unique designs, a wide range of official publications, books and magazines and Craft and Arch regalia. (Other regalia can be obtained to order.) It offers a range of items which can be personalised for individuals, Lodges or Chapters.

Letchworth's
Freemasons' Hall,
60 Great Queen Street
London
WC2B 5AZ
Tel: 020 7395 9329
Fax: 020 7404 7418
E-mail: info@letchworthshop.co.uk
www.letchworthshop.co.uk

Organisers of Ladies' Festivals and Masonic Balls

Square Events
This company endeavours to make "your special event the toast of your Lodge" – organised by Freemasons for Freemasons.
Square Events Management
184 Staines Road East
Sunbury on Thames
Middlesex
TW16 5AY
Tel: 01932 783877
E-mail: info@squareeventsmanagement.com
www.squareeventsmanagement.com

Ladies' Night Gifts

Letchworth's Shop at Freemasons' Hall (details above)
The Freemason (details above)

Sparkles by Suzi
This website offers Masonic Forget-me-not Swarovski Crystal earrings and necklaces. *www.sparklesbysuzi.co.uk/forget_me_not_masonic_jewellery.html*

Other useful information

RMBI Homes

Albert Edward, Prince of Wales Court, Porthcawl	01656 785311
Barford Court, Hove	01273 777736
Cadogan Court, Exeter	01392 251436
Connaught Court, York	01904 626238
Cornwallis Court, Bury St Edmunds	01284 768028
Devonshire Court, Oadby	0116 2714171
Ecclesholme, Eccles	0161 788 9517
Harewood Court, Hove	01273 739515
James Terry Court, Croydon	020 8688 1745
Lord Harris Court, Wokingham	0118 978 7496
Prince Edward, Duke of Kent Court, Braintree	01376 345534
Prince George, Duke of Kent Court, Chislehurst	020 8467 0081
Prince Michael of Kent Court, Watford	01923 234780
Queen Elizabeth Court, Llandudno	01492 877276
Scarborough Court, Cramlington	01670 712215
Shannon Court, Hindhead	01428 604833
The Tithebarn, Liverpool	0151 924 3683
Zetland Court, Bournemouth	01202 769169

The United Grand Lodge of England runs a scheme to promote and encourage Freemasonry among undergraduates and other university members. If you are a current student or an alumnus of a university, you may well find that there is a specific Lodge associated with your institution.

The scheme is gradually expanding to take in more university cities. A list of participating universities can be obtained on request from the following email address: universitiesscheme@email.com

Recommended Reading

Useful Titles for New Masons

Book of Constitutions of the United Grand Lodge of England – Includes two free booklets: 1. Information for the Guidance of Members of the Craft; 2. Information about Masonic Charities

Emulation First Degree Only Ritual – The Emulation Lodge of Improvement, Lewis Masonic
The perfect gift for the newly made Mason, providing him with an authoritative grounding in Masonic symbolism and practice and everything he needs for his next degree.

Emulation Second Degree Only Ritual – The Emulation Lodge of Improvement, Lewis Masonic
The perfect gift for the newly made Fellow Craft, providing him with an authoritative grounding in Masonic symbolism and practice and everything he needs for his next degree.

Emulation Ritual Revised Edition – The Emulation Lodge of Improvement, Lewis Masonic
This book contains the Official Emulation version of the Three Degrees of Craft Freemasonry and the installation ceremony with notes and guidelines on ritual procedure and practice Emulation Lectures of the Three Degrees. The most detailed and authoritative text on the true meaning of the Masonic rituals.

Making Light: A Handbook for Freemasons – Julian Rees, Lewis Masonic
A step-by-step guide to the path of self knowledge and self improvement that is Freemasonry.

Masonic Mnemonics – David Royal, Lewis Masonic
Fun and easy rhymes, jokes and anachronism that help you remember the order of Masonic procedure takes the pain out of learning Masonic ritual.

The Real Secrets of Freemasonry – Geoff Gibson, Lewis Masonic
Younger Brethren particularly and maybe those of retirement age will derive guidance and encouragement from the simple truths set out in this book, which should prove a source of help to them in their Masonic and everyday life.

Beyond The Craft – Keith B Jackson, Lewis Masonic
This guidebook details Masonic Orders beyond the Craft that are still worked in England and Wales.

The Stairway to Freemasonry – Julian Rees, Lewis Masonic
For any enquiring mind, whether Freemason or not, this little book sets out to help answer questions – not so much "What does it mean?" but rather, "What can it mean?"

Workman Unashamed: the Testimony of a Christian Freemason – Christopher Haffner, Lewis Masonic
Written from the heart, in a clear and well constructed manner, this book clearly demonstrates the compatibility of Freemasonry and Christianity.

A Daily Advancement in Masonic Knowledge – Ray Hollins, The Stechford Lodge No 3185
A series of lectures to increase the knowledge of the existing Mason.

A Masonic Miscellany – George Power, The Freemason Ltd
Titbits of Masonic trivia together with moral and inspiring quotes and stories.

Freemasonry for Dummies – Christopher Hodapp, John Wiley & Sons
A plain English introduction to the ancient organisation – a key to the history, beliefs and rituals of Freemasonry.

Handbooks for the Officers

The EA's Handbook – J. S. M. Ward, Lewis Masonic
The FC's Handbook – J. S. M. Ward, Lewis Masonic
The MM's Handbook – J. S. M. Ward, Lewis Masonic
The Assistant Officers: A Practical Guide – Richard Johnson, Lewis Masonic
The Principal Officers: A Practical Guide – Richard Johnson, Lewis Masonic
A Handbook for the Worshipful Master – Frank Rich, Lewis Masonic
A Guide to the Tyler's Work – Duncan Adams, Lewis Masonic
The Lodge Almoner – Charles J. Carter, Lewis Masonic
The Lodge Secretary – Charles J. Carter, Lewis Masonic
The Masonic Treasurer – A.W. Nelson, Lewis Masonic
The Duties and Responsibilities of the Director of Ceremonies – Jack Bright, Lewis Masonic
The Wardens, the Chaplain, the Immediate Past Master – Charles J. Carter, Lewis Masonic

Humorous titles

How Many Freemasons does it take to Change a Light Bulb? – Martin Faulks, Lewis Masonic
Do you believe that Freemasonry should be fun? If so, then this is the book for you! A handy compilation of Masonic jokes and one-liners that fits easily into your pocket.

Masonic Humour Vol. 1 – Jack Bright, Lewis Masonic
A collection of amusing tales and jokes from the world of Freemasonry and beyond. Useful to dip into for some light relief and as a source of ideas when speaking at the Festive Board.

More Jokes for Toasts – Jack Bright, Lewis Masonic
Non-Masonic jokes, useful for speeches and festivals.

Tied to Masonic Apron Strings – Stewart M. L. Pollard, Macoy Publishing
A book loaded with rib-ticklers; just the gift to speed recovery of an ailing Brother.

Index